XCZ.4.00 E

Dance

A CREATIVE ART EXPERIENCE

DANCE

A CREATIVE
ART EXPERIENCE

By

Margaret N. H'Doubler

With

DANCE SKETCHES BY
WAYNE L. CLAXTON

THE UNIVERSITY OF WISCONSIN PRESS

Published 1940, 1957

The University of Wisconsin Press
Box 1379, Madison, Wisconsin 53701
The University of Wisconsin Press, Ltd.
70 Great Russell Street, London

Printings 1957, 1959, 1962, 1966, 1968, 1972, 1974

Printed in the United States of America

ISBN 0-299-01520-3 cloth, 0-299-01524-6 paper
LC 57-7820

TO BLANCHE M. TRILLING

Who gave me inspiration, and whose vision and faith in the educational values of dance have made my work possible

Foreword

In a day and age when machines have all but conquered the world, and when man, the maker, has become the slave of his own inventions, it is not strange that we find education almost as regimented and pigeonholed as the humans who administer it. Our great factories of learning, our "free" education, have been adapted to the public which pays for them, and the materialistic demands of that public largely dominate their concepts. Creative activities, unless they lead to something called "pure science," have little chance of encouragement, though we hear much of "progressive education."

Despite all this, humanity remains much the same in its essential urges, and young men and young women in our great colleges and universities and elsewhere still know the inner urge to develop and reshape their powers of expression into some new and better form. Too few educators or educational institutions yet realize that, only by fostering and developing creative activities of mind and body, permitting each student to participate in some degree, and according to his own endowments, in creative activity and expression, can we hope to renew the much-needed spiritual aspects of our life today.

It is with some of these thoughts in mind that we turn to the work of the educator whose leadership in her field this book embodies. As a fellow faculty member I have watched her work in its study, example, precept, and practice since its inception in the University of Wisconsin. Beginning at a time when dance held literally no place or thought of place in the educational plan

FOREWORD

of any academic institution in the country, the author, Margaret H'Doubler, has been chiefly instrumental in bringing dance to its present state, where it is recognized as an educational factor in a great number of schools and colleges.

She more than any other one person has helped to remove dance from the realm of an applied activity, intended for a somewhat aesthetically inclined few among the students of any given institution, to its place as an accepted educational, scientific, artistic, and, above all, creative unit in the lives of students in our present collegiate setup.

That her tireless energy, keen intellect, and wide study have made advanced academic degrees attainable for students in dance is, in the last analysis, not to be compared in importance to the possibilities released through creative growth of mind and body. The hundreds of students who have gone out from her classes to carry further the ideas of dance in the educational scheme or elsewhere are the finest witnesses a great teacher and leader in any field may hope to have.

Only great minds can lead to greatness, to release, and to creation. Such a mind is the author of this book.

GERTRUDE E. JOHNSON
Associate Professor Emeritus
University of Wisconsin

Preface

In essence, *Dance: a Creative Art Experience* is a discussion of the basic aspects and enduring qualities of dance, which are within the reach of everyone. Its main purpose is to set forth a theory and a philosophy that will help us to see dance scientifically as well as artistically. In this respect it parallels certain phases of my earlier book, *Dance and Its Place in Education.* In a few instances material from the earlier book has been included here in an expanded form. But the purposes of the two are different.

Many excellent books concerning professional dancers and their contributions to the art have recently been published. For this reason, and because there seems to be a need for a presentation of dance from a more general point of view, there are several of its aspects which I do not attempt to cover. There are no descriptions of dances; there is no discussion of trends as such. Nor is there any reference to individual dancers whether of yesterday or of today.

Rather, this book is designed to show that dance is available to all if they desire it and that it is an activity in which some degree of enjoyment and aesthetic satisfaction for all may be found. If we can think, feel, and move, we can dance. In presenting dance from this point of view I have made an attempt to show its nature and conditions. From a knowledge of these conditions the reader may evaluate for himself the trends in contemporary dance; he may distinguish according to his own understanding between those phases that are evanescent and those that are lasting.

If dance is to be brought into universal use, if it is to help in the development of a more general appreciation of human art values, it must be considered educationally. The future of dance as a democratic art activity rests with our educational system. Not everyone can avail himself of studio training, and even those who can afford such training will find that few studios are interested in this aspect of dance. One of the ways dance can reach everyone is through the schools. Expression through spontaneous bodily activity is as natural to the child as breathing. This inborn tendency to expressive movement provides a reliable equipment with which to build a vocabulary for artistic dance expression. If every child in every school from his entrance until his graduation from high school or college were given the opportunity to experience dance as a creative art, and if his dancing kept pace with his developing physical, mental, and spiritual needs, the enrichment of his adult life might reach beyond any results we can now contemplate.

Dance considered from this standpoint can be of great social value, but to achieve these results we must bring it within the reach of the laity. It must be a vitalizing experience to them. Dance's power of civilization has always been felt whenever it has been experienced as a control over life in giving artistic form to its expression. This element has proven to be an enduring and vitally important power in the cultural life of all ages. It is for us today to rediscover this power and seek its influence. Only when dance is communally conceived can it exert a cultural influence.

When a people possesses such a dance spirit, many artists will rise from the ranks to carry dance to its highest unfoldment. Without this broad knowledge and belief, our artists will be few. The development of genius needs a sympathetic and understanding public just as much as the public needs the artist to realize and give back its dreams. As a growing and struggling art, dance needs above all the philosopher-scientist-artist, and he in turn needs a sympathetic public informed on the values and meaning of art.

MARGARET N. H'DOUBLER
Professor Emeritus
Department of Physical Education for Women
University of Wisconsin

Acknowledgment

In the attempt to assemble and put down in writing my thoughts and convictions concerning a subject that has long been one of study, thought, constant reading, observation, discussion, and active teaching, I cannot help realizing the many sources to which I am indebted for inspiration and assistance. There is the patient co-operation of students; the tolerance and sympathy of fellow department members; the stimulation of former teachers; the broad-mindedness of the administration of the University of Wisconsin in giving dance the dignity of a major course; the helpfulness of friends in preparing this manuscript; and finally the art of those dancers who have done so much to bring dance before the American public To all these I extend sincere acknowledgment.

Sincere thanks and appreciation are expressed to Professor and Mrs. Walter R. Agard, Professor and Mrs. Charles Bunn, and Dr. and Mrs. Erwin R. Schmidt for the loan of their drawings for reproduction in this new edition.

CONTENTS

Dance as an expression of the society it represents; its growth, from the early expressive but random movements of primitive man, to a consciously created art form, satisfying man's aesthetic sense.

Art as creative expression has its source within man's physical, mental, and emotional structure; dance therefore is the heritage of all mankind.

The need for creative art activity in the educational system; how dance fulfills this need.

The psychophysical-anatomical structure and its relation to movement and dance; training the mind to use the body as an expressive instrument; training the body to be responsive to the expressive mind.

CONTENTS

Introduction

To be born and be active and alive is to be endowed with a quickening "life-force" that animates us throughout our individual lives. The direction this force takes is to protect and preserve life, and to propagate its kind, manifesting behavior of moving toward or away from, with or against the forces that exist in man's environment. Thus life's experiencing comes from the interaction between man and nature—man and his social world, man and himself. In this interaction human energy is gathered and released, resulting in experiences that exalt us and depress us. There are rhythmic pulsations that run the emotional gamut from achievement to failure, from hope to despair, each with its own defining characteristics of tension and movement. Individual endowment rounds this all out into a unique thinking, feeling, active self. In the process man has and will continue to civilize himself. Thus life becomes a drama of adjustment to the conditions of existence. All that man has accomplished has been executed by bodily movement. The very fact that man is endowed with effective stepping movements and can go places has been and always will be influential in the cultural advancement of the human mind as well as an assurance of man's survival.

Whoever undertakes the guidance of this "life-force," whether the parent in the home or the teacher in the schoolroom or the artist in his studio, should feel the necessity of obtaining as much knowledge as is possible of its devious ways of expression as revealed in the various stages of growth from infancy to adulthood

INTRODUCTION

The necessity to live is a basis of unrest. It leads to a kind of activity that manifests purpose, a working toward the restoration of harmony with environment or self, as the case may be.

To help understand human behavior, we have scientific knowledge to give understanding of man's biological and psychological natures, as well as of his environment. In seeking a biologic understanding of man, we do not go to science to become scientists, but to gain that kind of knowledge which gives informed appreciation of the living processes that animate our activities. Every individual to grow into psychological maturity needs some basic knowledge of human responses and of the dependency of all behavior on inborn drives. He needs to understand himself as a sensitive, reacting, changing organism. This is a concern of the mental equipment which determines psychic behavior.

Scientific knowledge can give us methods of tapping human and physical resources and valid ways of dealing with the more factual quantitative aspects of experience. They are constant and unchanging. But in no way does science profess to explain the more subtle, feeling, intuitive aspects. These are the qualitative considerations of experience. Although intangible, they have a reality of their own, and exist as powerful and necessary drives to compel us to action. Scientific knowledge, therefore, can help us to appreciate the great wealth of human and natural resources. But we go to the humanities for our cultural knowledges— philosophy, religion, and art—to give us understanding of how, through the different stages of civilization, mankind has found values and meanings to give significance to life. With more knowledge and experience, new values are found, and in the process emotional values and interest shift, resulting in various stages of culture.

And finally, there are the art knowledges to help us understand the eternal need of man to order, express, and communicate his appreciation of truth and beauty as he sees them.

These are knowledges which are of value to all persons. Important as professional knowledges are to a teacher, a general cultural background is essential to serve as a rich storehouse of source material with which to solicit the varied interests and feeling responses of the students. For emotional guidance and growth is education's responsibility as well as to impart factual knowledge.

Everyone, from his own experience, knows something about feeling states, but may not be very appreciative of the important role they play in life. We cannot ignore or isolate ourselves from the emotional forces of our nature, for they are among the most basic and deeply rooted and biologically useful forms of behavior. We have survived because of them and they make life worth living. They mobilize all our energies, physical and psychical, for action and in the process the total self is unified.

A complete understanding of the emotional nature is still in the process of development, but it is quite generally agreed that the awareness of an emotion is preceded by the perception of a stimulating event, recognizing it for what it is worth to the self. Is it beneficial or harmful? Is it significant or meaningless? The judgment or evaluation will depend on the knowledge and experience one has concerning the exciting event or similar experiences. It is the interpretative decision which serves as the signal for the body to get into action. The awareness of the body's readiness for action, a tension caused by deep-seated physical changes, is the emotion. At this point, understanding and reason can intervene and condition the reflex acts of the primary nature and bring them under conscious control. When this occurs, movements manifest discrimination and personal choice. If behavior were entrusted entirely to the untutored reflex acts of the primary nature and were to serve only its biological protests, there could be little or no advancement in the culture of the individual or in civilization.

The emotions are a phase of man's natural endowment which needs understanding and guidance. To bring the emotional nature under control does not mean that the emotions are to be suppressed. If that were true, why the emotions? It means that their motivating force needs to be harnessed and guided into behavior of constructive purpose. With self-knowledge comes self-direction and security, because knowledge makes individual judgment and choice possible, thus breaking down inhibitions, and clearing the way for effective creative effort. Because of the inescapable relation between feeling and movement, knowledge of the emotional nature can be gained through the study of movement as a medium of creative experience and expression.

Unfortunately, the word creative is too often considered as a special endowment bestowed only upon artists, or as something belonging to genius, instead of an innate capacity possessed by everyone. When the least endowed are permitted to carry creative effort to its simplest production, it can be as psychologically satisfying as the effort of the more talented.

INTRODUCTION

To want to create something is the result of a sensed need to arrange already existing materials into forms that meet the individual's standards. Creative activity combines what knowledge we have of a stimulating event with that of our relationship to it. It is this self-identification with experience that is the very core of creative effort. To teach by means of creative thinking and doing is to tap the resources of students and guide them into channels of productivity which are their own. When creativity is the issue, much depends upon the teacher's ability to inspire confidence in the students so that they will be unafraid of what they might reveal when honestly expressing their own reactions. This interrelationship implies creative effort on the part of both teacher and student. To find new meanings and to give new forms to the values found is life's creative principle of adjustment. It is an inherent and biological principle before it is an art principle.

Art cannot be divorced from life—it is of life's essence. The central subject matter of all art is emotional value not fact. The art which expresses emotional values in movement is dance. So to dance one must study and explore and know movement.

To know movement, one must move and attend to the sensations of his own moving body, thereby discovering movement to be a highly stimulating experience whose sensations can be held in consciousness where they can be recognized, compared, evaluated, and where ideas can be formed about them. Because we are endowed with a kinesthetic sense, we can perceive the relative degree of speed and force of muscle tension with which a movement is being performed. We can also perceive the duration of the performed movement and the changing spatial relationship between the moving body parts, and between the body and other objects in space. Also, kinesthetic perception is the basis of rhythmic perception whereby the rhythmic structure of a movement can be perceived and analyzed. These judgments of duration and force are the basis for further judgments of effort present in all activities. To be educated movementwise should mean the ability to appropriate and modify the instinctive motor responses into consciously selected and disciplined effective acts.

Heightened kinesthetic perception is the only reliable guide to such a critical awareness and self-discipline. It is our observable behavior that reveals our relationship to events which happen to us. And it is in the performed acts that we discover the self through knowledge gained from the effects of our own acts. The body is not the total person. We possess it, but we live in our acts. Movement sensations within themselves have no feeling. The subjective, affective phase of the movement experience is the perception of the movement sensations and the associative feeling states and ideas aroused by them. The affective phase of movement (its power to evoke thought and feeling) is the important issue in studying movement preparatory for dance as an art form. To attend to the sensations of movement, to concentrate on its rhythmic structure, and to operate under an understanding of their significance is to have a creative art experience. Such a creative experience brings the total personality into an integrated action. Rhythm, because it is the law of muscle action, permeates the whole organism and unites it into a unified whole. It controls the flow of all our energies, and its effects are felt as organized and harmonious.

The creative process is a coöperative activity: of the intellect, in constructing form; of the emotions, the motivating force for expression; of the body, whose active joints (the skeletal instrument) and muscles (the movement medium) furnish the materials for the organized external form; and finally of that intangible aspect of human personality, the spirit, which animates these activities with greater significance. A created dance is born of the personality. In creating external form, the personality is expanded in achieving a form of expression and communication. Thus the personality is active in its entirety.

Unfortunately, because of the lack of movement education, the average person is kinesthetically unaware of movement as a source of self-awareness and well-being; therefore movement cannot play its important role in the life of the individual. The inherent relationship between thought, feeling, and action furnishes the basis and direction for a procedure of creative teaching and learning. And it is the awareness of their inseparability in the totally functioning human organism which forms the basis of a concept of dance as a truly educational experience. Movement experiences need to be presented in such a way that the student will be able to summon and integrate his intellectual, emotional, and physical responses, and in this way be able to identify himself with his own movement experience. Such movement participation is both active and passive, for while one is executing a movement (active phase) the movement is doing something to him in return (passive phase) because of the "feed-back" of movement sensations to the central nervous system. In this double experience the student gains knowledge not only of himself as a moving object but also of himself as a sensitive, feeling, knowing self—a subjective-objective interactivity. How much more important for students to become motorly adaptable and personally secure in their knowledge of movement than to depend upon the opinions and movements of others! When the idea becomes clear in the student's own thinking, he has constructed it for himself and it is his, although the impetus for thinking had its source in another.

The knowledge of kinesthesia and the deepening knowledge of movement and rhythm and of the relation between feeling and its movement expression are trends which are influencing the development of dance today. More emphasis is being placed on developing techniques according to forms that are inherent in movements because of body structure and function, rather than techniques developed for visual appearance alone. A change in the technical study of dance, naturally, brings about a change in its theory and philosophy—and vice versa. As a result dance today is accepted as a creative art form, expressing and communicating the dancer's values as he knows them. The concept of contemporary dance is not a prescribed system; it is dance conceived in terms of all that we know today of its science, its philosophy, and its claim to art. Perhaps it might be helpful, and cause less confusion, to think of our students as modern youth dancing, instead of their performing "modern dance." For after all, any art form is modern in its time. Dance today is the contemporary phase of dance in its development toward greater universality.

In dance, movement as the medium evokes feeling states; it does not release them. It is true that in an emotional reaction the muscle tensions, resulting in bodily movement, are the medium of release resulting in expressive behavior revealing the emotional nature. But this is not dance as art. Art creates the image; it does not reproduce reality. The value of art discipline, a formative process, lies in the ability to objectify emotion. To objectify an emotion is to remove it from its original experience and to evaluate it for its uniqueness. By means of the art act, the individual can aesthetically experience the emotion within the art form he has created instead of reliving it in its original situation. In dance, the dancer reflects through bodily tensions and disciplined movements the emotion and meaning he wishes to communicate, but without involving himself as a person. And again, movement becomes dance when the feelings aroused by movement are the reason for moving. Movement thus is the source of meaning as well as the medium for expressing and communicating its own meaning. This means that, when he is dancing, the dancer's movements communicate back to him, and he must be constantly aware of them and their effect on him. If the dancer is not stimulated by the truth and beauty of his movements, there will be no communication either to the dancer or to an audience, if an audience is included. This kind of concentration is the secret of projection. Both the dancer and the audience must be aroused to an aesthetic reaction. The "feed-back" into consciousness completes the creative integrating act.

Thus dance may be considered a neural projection of inner

thought and feeling into movement, rhythm being the mold through which the creative life flows in giving its meaning form. The vitalizing and revitalizing effect of creative effort and production is the ultimate value of any creative art experience. Through creative experience one's acts come to have significance for the self, the basis of character.

Dance in education does not exist just for the pleasure of dancing, but through creative effort in giving aesthetic forms to significant experience it is hoped students will develop their creative power and in turn improve themselves as persons. Creative ability has many applications to life and can contribute much to improve the quality of living. It is a means of becoming sensitive to quality values in one's environment, not only as found in the arts, but also as they can be observed in nature and human relations. Because of the nature of creative effort, participation in it can contribute to a heightened and critical awareness of life, not only in evaluating experiences, but also in creating the forms of their expression.

Students bring a wealth of natural endowment to a study of movement. They come with a structure made for action, another for its perception and control, a rich inheritance of reaction patterns, and an innate love to move. What are we doing with this endowment? Nature adequately provides the means for self-expression through movement; education must provide the ways. Not until provision is made in the curriculum for creative activities can we hope to renew much-needed aesthetic sensitivity in our lives today and be freed from herd-like conformity.

To integrate one's self within a group, and coöperate intelligently with his fellow men, one first must feel the security and self-value which comes from integration within the self. Self-understanding is the basis of understanding other selves. The individual's culture as well as the culture of the social order is dependent upon man's ability to create and produce. These are human qualities which must be saved. To release and foster creativity is one of education's greatest challenges.

Chapter 1
A CULTURAL SURVEY OF DANCE

Man fashions as he knows.

EVERY AGE has had its dance, and the fact that dance has lived is evidence of its value. The universal interest in dance rests upon the fact that it carries on and systematizes an activity that is operative in everyone's experience. It is co-existent with life.

Like the history of all the arts, the history of dance follows those changes in attitude and feeling and those fluctuations in man's concept of art which have given to every period its distinctive qualities. Its history therefore is one of changes in those points of view by which man has built his ideals rather than a chronicle of techniques and forms.

The very nature of dance—the living, pulsating movement whose path is closed as the path of an arrow—makes a true history impossible. By reason of its nature, a dance remains only in the visual memory of the onlooker and in the kinesthetic memory of the dancer. For a dance to exist, immediacy of motor response to the mental life of the dancer is required. In dancing, as in acting, the artist must be present in the full possession of his personality.

The interest in recording dances is evidenced by the many efforts of those who have studied this problem. We read of methods of recording dances (orchesography) that date as far back as the Egyptians and the Greeks. It would be interesting to know how successful their methods were. The more recent efforts either to revive ancient methods or to invent new ones have so far been ineffectual for general use. However, the rhythmical structure of a dance, and its design and spatial pattern, can be quite satisfactorily recorded. This recording is useful as a recall for its creator and as a form stimulus for other dancers. But the most important elements of expression, the subtle and personal nuances, which so clearly reflect the emotional conditions and artistic intention of the dancer, cannot be so reproduced. In short, it is impossible for such an art medium as dance to be preserved as a form through the ages, for its very nature lacks the elements necessary to permanency. It may be, however, that in the future the motion picture will furnish some sort of solution to this problem.

Space will not permit a thorough and detailed account of dance from its crude beginnings to its present development. Indeed, the scope of dance is so vast that to attempt a brief survey seems futile. Although such a study is closely related to our subject, it seems more pertinent to glance at the high points of man's cultural evolution and to try to gain some understanding of how dance came to be what it is, to observe the conditions under which it existed, and to note in passing the place it held in man's group and individual life. For this reason there is no attempt at classification or description of specific dances.

Primitive

The earliest expressive acts of man could have been none other than random, impulsive movements, unorganized except as they followed the natural laws of his functioning body structure. They were probably characterized by a passion for rhythm. Later in his development man acquired a group status. He began to realize that groups could live and work together with greater results than lone individuals could achieve. Gradually he came to feel himself

4

part of a larger unit, and this feeling must have had both a restraining and a stimulating effect upon his activities. His individual desire gave way to group customs, and his dancing began to reflect a widening range of human circumstances and adventure. He still danced his love, fear, hate, and anger, but with a difference—his dancing being regulated by the consciousness of his identity with a group.

History informs us that in these early human societies, dance derived its major importance from its function as an integral part of the social and religious life. For primitive man there was no such thing as religion apart from life. Religion *was* life—it included everything. It was but natural that these dances dealt very directly with all the different phases of life. Since all important events in the life cycle of the individual had both a practical and a religious significance, they were symbolized in bodily movement. The result is a wide variety of dances, which may be reduced to three main groups—the religious dances, the dramatic presentations of love and war, and the imitative dances devoted to the mimicry of animals, of forces of nature, and of gods. All three groups were pantomimic and were entered into for the purpose of heightening individual and group states of feeling and of initiating for magical reasons various natural processes. In this way the dancer was enabled to enter the realm of superbeings. The auto-intoxication of rapturous movement brought him into a self-forgetful union with the not-self that the mystic seeks.

Primitive life is exultant. It loves to jump and yell and fling its arms and legs about. Early man communicated his belief in the gods and the experiences of his own daily life by stamping, clapping, swaying, shouting, grunting, and crying, with noise as well as with motion. Young life also loves to imitate and make believe, and this love of pretense, along with man's innate urge to express what he feels, is the chief motive from which dance, music, song, poetry, and drama develop as independent expressive arts.

Early man did not know he was making art. He was only projecting in movement and sound his feelings, wants, and needs, expressing his daily life and his belief in his gods. He had no other escape for his pent-up feelings than the movements of his own body. So he danced.

It is doubtful, however, whether the earliest art forms were created consciously to satisfy man's aesthetic sense, and it would be impossible to say just when his creative impulse, instinctive and unverbalized, first led him consciously to fashion beautiful forms for their own sake. When we remember how undeveloped was the mind of early man, and how rigorous were the conditions in which he lived, we can understand that his earliest forms of expression were, of necessity, very close to his life's needs, and that these forms were crude and utilitarian in their nature.

Thus we learn that primitive man danced under the influence of strong excitement, and for personal pleasure, using mimetic gestures by which he told a tale or mocked a rival. To him dance was magic motion by which he could influence the great forces of nature around him. It served as a means to propitiate the gods and thus secure happiness. At this stage dance was largely instinctive and spontaneous in its forms, serious and utilitarian in its purpose, and tremendously religious and social in value. It is in the life of primitive society that we recognize the tremendous power of dance as a socializing influence.

As the human race advanced, man became more and more conscious of his environment. Both group and individual differentiations appeared. Tribes became nations. Man gained wider experience, learned to discriminate, and grew in power of reflection. Thought and observation developed characteristic beliefs, scientific systems, and ethical schemes. As man's powers of perception strengthened, he became more and more enlightened, and again we find the intellectual and social change reflected in dance.

Ancient

Conditions became such that the need for the early socializing influence of dance was no longer felt. Man was finding other channels through which to communicate his thoughts and feelings. Music and poetry became the chief language of the emotions. Dance, however, showed no tendency to die out. As man's faculties developed subtleties of observation and discrimination, the primitive religious dancing gradually became crystallized into the religious dramas and ritualistic dances of the ancient civilizations. As his mental life increased in complexity, intellect began to dominate the emotions. He learned restraint and choice. As a result, a new actuating force entered the impulse to dance. Aesthetic reasons for dancing appeared. It is not likely that primitive man sought these elements consciously, although they are inherent in his forms of expression. Nor is it likely that he was

DANCE: A CREATIVE ART EXPERIENCE

at first concerned with a nicety of results. It would be difficult to state just when nonaesthetic motives ended and aesthetic motives began. But art history reports to us that all forms and developments of art are and always have been witness to an activity which tends to become more and more independent of the immediate utilities of life.

We might say, then, that in the dances of ancient civilizations thought was combined with dramatic intent, and aesthetic elements were consciously sought. Indeed, we read of instances where these elements were even controlled by law. The result was the curbing of any tendency to excessive emotion. This development led to a ritualistic formalism so great that special knowledge is necessary to catch its significance.

Dance remained rich in meaning but became more moderate and beautiful in form. It was no longer so natural, so directly connected with daily activities. Ritualistic formality existed side by side with imagination and frenzy. The same themes of religion, love, and war persisted. We also read of dancing for the purpose of attaining agility and grace. The cultured ancients considered dance an art and raised it to a place of high esteem.

The value of dance to individual development, although manifesting itself throughout the lower stages of civilization, was not fully realized until the *Athenian* civilization. With these Greeks, dance again played an important role and became a deliberate feature of a philosophic scheme of education.

The Athenian point of view held that life in this world was all that mattered, and that it should be lived as abundantly and beautifully as was humanly possible. The philosophic Greeks had none of the Christian fear of God. They worshiped beauty and sought beauty in every phase of their mental, emotional, and physical life, but their ideal was that in nothing should man go to excess. All that enlightened man did was to be tempered by a delicate appreciation of taste and moderation. The Greeks revered especially the beauty of the human form. Its perfect development was to them an expression of the soul within, and dance was the embodiment of its rhythm, harmony, proportion, and balance, which were the very foundations of their moral life. Thus to the Greek of the age of Pericles, living in itself became an art; for he was ever seeking proportionate and harmonious relations in all that he was capable of thinking, feeling, and doing. The place that dance held in such a civilization is obvious. Not only was it deemed essential to the development of taste and refinement, but it was also considered a necessary part of military and religious training. For a citizen to be well educated, he must sing and dance well, and to sing and dance well meant to sing and dance only that which was good. Consequently, dance was regarded as one of the best aids to man's development. As one of the highest cultural expressions of art, it at once revealed and enriched man's spirit.

Of course, such a conception could be the fruit only of the philosophy of the enlightened few. Through the working of a long-established tradition of mental and spiritual refinement they had become attuned to its spirit. Such an ideal as this, transplanted to foreign soil, was doomed to perish.

As we pass from the best of Greek civilization down through

its decline in the Roman period, we see that this is what happened. When the Romans, in the course of their conquests, came into contact with Greek civilization, they were impressed by its elegance. To them it was all very novel and interesting, for art had long flourished in Greece, whereas Rome was still barbaric. The Romans coveted the riches of Greek culture and tried to make them their own. But Greek art was the fruit of a philosophy and an attitude toward life which the Romans could neither understand nor appreciate. The fundamental difficulty was that the Greek view of life was aesthetic, and the Roman was not. The Greeks lived their dances; the Romans copied their forms. As a result, the exaltations expressed through the bodily power of the Greeks became licentious in the hands of the Romans. Dance became a source of entertainment, indulged in more for sensual delight than for an expression of the artistic nature. The Romans did not find in the human form a revelation of the spiritual realm; they saw only the body in the body.*

Moreover, the dance which the Romans cultivated was not a dance peculiar to them and evolved by them; it was a dance that was peculiar to the development of another people. It was not an expression of the Roman spirit, nor could the Roman populace understand its beauty. Dance became so debased that it was looked down upon by the Roman philosophers as an amusement unfit for the cultured. Even though theatrical and mimetic dancing reached

---

* It must be remembered that the Roman Empire, as a conquering state, was subject to the sensualities of its varied and foreign inhabitants, a condition which may be considered as one of the factors that caused the art forms of the more cultured Greeks to perish.

a high stage of perfection among the Romans, dance as art fell with the decay of their civilization. The fault did not lie in dance. It was the use made of it. Because movement so truthfully reflects feeling, it has always been a mirror of the moral attitude of peoples. Just as language may be expressive either of vulgar or of refined thought and feeling, so movement may be either pleasing or repulsive.

The fall of the Graeco-Roman culture is generally thought of as marking the decline of ancient civilization. The disintegration of ancient social, political, and economic institutions that followed created a religious need of a more individual and emotional nature than was possible in the formalized Roman state religion. During Rome's declining years the Mediterranean world became drained of its energies. People were ready to accept peace and security at any cost.

Such was the state of mind that made possible the introduction of Christianity and the transformation of the Roman Empire into a Christian empire. With the appearance and acceptance of Christianity, mankind was confronted with a complete change in philosophy. Emphasis of life values became transferred from this world to the life of the hereafter, and the spiritual rather than the material world was thought the more important.

Medieval

The foregoing is a brief statement of the background that laid the foundation of the emerging cultural synthesis called *medievalism*. Our focus of attention now shifts from the Mediterranean world to continental Europe, since it was western Europe that was destined as a frontier world to affect the culture of our country. Medieval Europe presents perhaps the most unified culture pattern the civilized world has ever known. It was a great unified structure whose religious hold upon its people may be compared in strength to that of early primitive cultures.

After the fall of the ancient Roman Empire, Europe was overrun with warring tribes and roaming peoples. There followed a turmoil of migrations, cultural changes, and conflicting religious and social currents. The great writers of Greece and Rome were forgotten, and the great centers of learning were destroyed. The early years of this period were indeed dark and illiterate. Greek philosophy failed to capture the masses of the Mediterranean, but Christianity succeeded. Both Greek and Egyptian religions were finally overcome by Christianity's powerful appeal as a scheme of life suited to the needs of men. The great need was spiritual uplift rather than intellectual development. Men preferred to be led rather than to think for themselves. They aspired not toward personal development and independence, but toward more security.

The Christian church with its far-reaching organization and its spiritual appeal arose at the psychological moment to succeed. Its unity and supremacy meant universal citizenship in the one church. Religion was the one controlling emotion. Outside the church allegiance was to landed overlords of the fast-spreading feudal system. Feudalism and the church, alike, demanded above everything else obedience to authority. Thought was dominated by the church, and the regulations of the feudal system forced the individual to submit to the common good, with no voice in determining what was the common good. Even if, in achieving this submission, the regime brought the evils of bigotry, cruelty, and suppression, it must be recognized that no other system could have brought the stability men so greatly needed.

The characteristic feature of early Christian thought was its otherworldliness. The emphasis was transferred from this world to the kingdom after death, and sharp distinctions were drawn not only between the here and the hereafter but also between good and evil, mind and body, spirituality and carnality. This attitude toward life was reflected in plays that originated among the clergy, the most important of which were the mystery, miracle, and morality plays that took their themes from Biblical sources. The paramount consideration of all living was to save the soul. Consequently, the body was looked upon as a hindrance. To exalt the soul the body was ignored, punished, and bruised. Anything that expressed the livelier feelings of instinctive human nature, or in any way suggested former pagan ways and ideals of living, was banished into the realm of wickedness. Dance, both because it was pleasurable and because it was physical, was frowned upon and all but suppressed in secular life, and was permitted to exist only in a staid form as a part of the ritual of worship.

This attitude was new. Primitive dancing had always possessed a central place in the religious life of all primitive and ancient races. The records of sacred meetings show that until the medieval period dancing had always been essential in vital religions; nor did the early Christians frown upon dancing. It was only when the early and simple teachings of Christ were distorted into a fanatical asceticism that dance, along with all the natural, healthy pleasures of man, fell into disfavor.

The Middle Ages saw the flowering of Christianity which inspired men to two great undertakings, the crusades and the building of cathedrals. Both were an expression of spiritual yearning, devotion, and sacrifice. However, it is in the light of the crusades that we read of the tragic persecution and wholesale slaughter of heretics.

The glorious medieval cathedrals were reared in the same spirit of devotion. Whole communities co-operated in their construction; everyone contributed what he could, from the farmer with his horses to the great painters and sculptors. There never was an architecture more original or more completely of the soil. The Gothic cathedral was the one art form that spoke for every class and condition of men.

This period also gave rise to universities. Although they were clerical and scholastic in outlook, they gave great impetus to intellectual development. Besides the scholars of the universities there were alchemists, astrologers, and magicians. Scholastic argument concerned itself mainly with the fundamentals of human thought as the medieval mind knew it. This discipline, coupled with the stern mental and moral training inspired by religious exaltation, yielded an extraordinary flowering of character and art.

One of the most interesting influences on art at this time was the rise of a lay culture. The rise of capitalism in turn gave rise to an industrial and commercial class which became a patron and leader of learning and art. Men once more became interested in this world instead of living in constant anticipation of the other. This secularized culture expressed itself in palaces, private residences, and paintings that were created to give men pleasure and enjoyment. In its effort to arrive at a more natural expression of the world and nature, art became independent of religious symbolism. This quest for a better understanding of the sensuous world was a direct outcome of knowledge that filtered through from the east during the crusades, and was also stimulated by contacts with other civilizations in the expansion of commerce. The unleashing of new intellectual forces presented to the church the problem of assimilating this new knowledge and bringing about an intellectual synthesis that would still be in keeping with its fundamental teachings and spirit. In art and literature an attempt was also made to bring about a harmony between the world of spiritual values and the world of nature. Thus medieval culture exhibits a strange contrast between the chivalrous ideals of knighthood and the coarse, barbaric conditions of life that supported it. It probably was the expression of the latter in the dances and brawls of the lower classes that caused the church to put a ban on dancing except when it was used in the church as a rhythmic processional form. This attitude is further revealed in sacred music, which in no way permitted the use of rhythms that would set the feet in motion.

But there is another side to medievalism. Its monkish bigotry, superstitions, religious fanaticism, sensuality, belief in witchcraft, pleasure in torture, and dancing manias reveal an unbalanced and uncontrolled mind. Men were possessed with the primitive fear of death. They lived in constant dread and contemplation of death in the midst of daily exposure to the ravages of war, famine, and plague. There was no conception of the consolations of death. They knew only its horrors and expressed their feelings in the concrete embodiment of death in its most gruesome aspects. The church offered possible consolation in righteous living. Death was personified as a skeleton to convey terrifying ideas about death's punishment for sin. There developed from this death complex a cultural folk drama in the allegorical pageants of the Dance of Death. The Dance of Death motive was a very popular theme of the writings and art of this period. Its basic theme—the leveling process that makes all men equal—has continued through the Renaissance to our times, each age expressing it according to its own philosophy.

The dancing mania that swept over Europe during and immediately after the Black Death was no new disease, but a phenomenon well known to the Middle Ages. Its appearance is thought to be due to a nervous disorder akin to imitative hysteria. The depleted physical and tortured mental conditions of the wretched populace, caused by war, famine, and pestilence, played a large part in conditioning their minds for the mental disorder that found relief in this demoniacal dancing epidemic. Men, women, and young boys and girls would dance in wild delirium, seemingly possessed and without any will of their own. Morbid

bystanders often became infatuated and would join in the bac-
chanalian frenzy. This dancing malady was known as St. Vitus'
or St. John's dance, according to the patron saint who was sup-
posed to protect the afflicted. In Italy the same disorder was called
tarantism, as it was at first thought to be caused by the bite of a
tarantula. But it was discovered that even those who were not
bitten contracted the disease, and the only explanation pointed to
a mental disorder.

In spite of the attitude of the medieval church, dance flourished
under the auspices of chivalry and became an important part of
the elaborate masquerades and balls given in the latter part of
the Middle Ages by the courts. It also achieved prominence in the
half-secularized morality plays of the medieval craft guilds.
Dance continued to play a prominent part in the festivities of the
people, and many of the dances were half pagan and half Christian
in origin. From these mixed sources dance may be said to have
continued its forward movement in two directions: that of the
highly conventionalized court dances, which were developed
further by professional dancers; and that of the healthy, freer,
more expressive folk dance, which all through the centuries had
grown up among the peasantry of the various countries. In spite
of the many changes in religious belief and the various social cri-
ses that followed through the centuries, it held its own in con-
tinuing to exist as a sincere expression of group life.

Gradually the medieval synthesis had to give way in its turn
to a new order and a new thought. As in the other civilizations, the
ways of the medieval world endured only as long as conditions

remained favorable for them, or as long as they satisfied men's needs. Many historical events conspired to break down this culture. New continents were discovered; new outlets for human energy arose; autocracy was challenged by the first revolutionary movements toward democracy; authority broke down under the challenge of criticism and science; the Reformation purged religion of its cramping absolutism; serfs became free workers. A social unrest was manifesting itself among the laboring classes and was augmented by the devastating Black Death, a plague that swept Europe in the middle of the fourteenth century and wiped out a large proportion of the population, including many of the landed aristocracy and those holding church and state offices. There was a shortage of labor, and offices had to be filled with whatever human material was left—all of which resulted in higher wages and in opportunities for the laboring classes to hold office. The printing press and the spreading use of gunpowder also made their contributions at this time to the liberation of men's thought and social freedom.

Renaissance

Men's thirst for knowledge grew with such force that the time came when all Europe seemed to rise to its feet and to champion the new order of learning and humanism. This new order, the *Renaissance,* marks the beginning of modern individualism, a spirit which has continued to grow and flourish through our own times. The new attitude of mind was mainly secular. Although a secular culture had arisen in the previous age, it was not until the

18

Renaissance that the laity actually assumed cultural leadership and established once and for all the idea that culture was a thing independent of religious interests.

The Renaissance world, it will be recalled, was an expression of renewed interest in the culture of the ancient world. Men sought to create a culture that would reflect the spirit of the Greek classics. This ideal was the moving force in the establishment of a type of school and education that was deemed essential to the cultured Christian gentleman. It was limited to the wealthy classes, who now became the patrons of both learning and art.

Another interesting feature of the Renaissance spirit was that art became less and less a group activity and more and more the creative product of individual artists. Private studios became the laboratories of technical experimentation where artists were free to develop their own new techniques of artistic expression and to throw off traditional conventions. Such was the cultural background that developed and nourished the conventional court dances and ballet of Renaissance Europe.

With the improvement of musical instruments in the seventeenth century, music entered into an instrumental era. Instrumental music, instead of song, became the popular accompaniment of dancing. Musicians early realized the value of combining contrasting dance forms into suites to get variety and mood in their music. In addition to the usual allemande, courante, saraband, and gigue, many other dances were used. They present themselves in a long list of familiar names, such as gavotte, bourrée, rigaudon, minuet, pavan, galliard, and polonaise. Some were slow, stately, restrained, and pompous; some were spirited, lively, and gay; and others were gliding and graceful. Each had its particular rhythm, some in duple time and some in triple time; and each had its special music, and continued in popularity as long as it pleased and satisfied the fickle whims of the court. With later developments came the waltz, mazurka, polka, and schottische.

These dances in most instances had their origins in folk forms, which were transposed into forms suitable for the court. Some were German, others French, Spanish, and Italian in their source. As they became conventionalized into court dances, the interest centered in technique rather than in the spirit or expressive value of the dance. Spontaneity and impulse were lost, and the two dance forms became widely separated in fundamental purpose. However, in their separate trends they existed side by side, and each continued to influence the other, the folk spirit generating vitality for new social forms, and the formalism of the aristocratic forms contributing a polishing influence to the cruder folk forms. The peasantry of rural communities continued to dance their feelings and to learn their inherited forms through observation and participation, whereas urban and aristocratic groups were told what to dance and how to dance it. Their steps, postures, and pantomimic gestures were the inventions and decisions of the professional dancing masters. The notable qualities of these dances were their artificiality and their demand for small precise movements rather than large instinctive ones. This, however, is not so true of the dances of the later Renaissance, where we meet such active dances as the polka and mazurka, and the graceful, gliding, more open movements of the waltz.

An explanation of the more stilted forms may lie in the costumes of the court, which did not permit freedom of movement, and in the court life, where the custom of doing nothing left men and women bored and avid for novel entertainment. The wealth and leisure of the nobility permitted long periods of study. They also made possible the hiring of professional dancers, who could be paid to demonstrate the elaborations and refinements of a highly studied technique. There was, therefore, a certain expressive relationship between the artificial dance and the artificialities of court life. The elaboration of technique made it unavailable except to a few, and the courtly habits of living, which were comparatively detached from the fundamental issues of life, made it impossible for these dances to have much richness of meaning.

The French ballet in the latter part of the seventeenth century ceased to be the pastime of amateurs and became the serious work of professional dancers. In 1661 the ballet as an art form entered the program of the newly established Académie Royale de Musique et du Danse, in Paris. Its objective and its claim to the title of art was the insistence on the perfection of technique. Little effort was made at expression; all vitality and spontaneity were sacrificed for the classical ideals of clarity and symmetry. As its principles and instruction became more pedantic, its movements became systematized and limited until finally all human impulse seemed lost to dance.

The ballet continued to use the age-old themes of legend, worship, nature, love, and combat, but they held no mystic or religious significance for the minds of the court and served only as entertainment and spectacle.

As the ballet became professional and divorced itself from amateur activity by going over to the theater, we had ballet produced for the entertainment of an audience whose interest was more often in the popular ballerina of the season than in the art values of dance. Between the emptiness and the artful complexity, dance inevitably degenerated in form and lost vitality, until finally these aristocratic dances no longer responded even to the narrow realities of court life—the life that gave them birth.

Parallel with the development of the ballet and other conventional forms, the folk dances grew up as a much more vital and expressive art. The term *folk dance* is used to distinguish the dance forms of the peasant classes from those of more cosmopolitan groups. Folk culture resembles primitive culture in its social character, for in neither do individuals have great importance as such. Men are born into folk ways and can do nothing but surrender themselves to those ways; individuals are cogs in the social machinery built up for efficiency and racial preservation. The folk culture was highly collective, and the customs of the folk were based not upon the development of individual personality but upon group living and group interests. In such a culture, the individual, being owned by the group and to a large extent identical with it in feeling, must have felt a deep allegiance to it and have delighted in expressing, through custom-regulated ceremonial, his own participation in group ideals and customs.

A CULTURAL SURVEY OF DANCE

Although the peasant dances of this later period reflected culture patterns different from those of primitive man, the quality of movement was on somewhat the same artistic level; both types of dance were a free expression of natural feeling. Both were the expression of peoples who had labored, fought, and lived together, and who, unhampered by self-consciousness, expressed their common joys and sorrows by natural rhythmic movement. But the folk dance reveals a great advancement in form as organization. Though the folk forms are exacting in a way, and though each generation has to learn from the preceding one, the movements themselves are natural and instinctive, allowing for abandonment and freedom of expression. They give the spirit full play without any premium on formal technique, and their appeal is that of directness, vigor, simplicity, and vitality. Folk dances give a convincing impression of being genuine and sound. They were meant to be shared and understood.

These qualities caused them to be almost instantly popular upon their introduction into American schools. Although folk dancing has to a large extent outgrown its original popularity, knowledge of folk forms is valuable, in fact essential, to a broad concept of dance.

The chief significance of the folk dance lies in two facts: it does not demand a highly developed skill for its performance and enjoyment, and it is not individualistic. Dance today must be individual as well as social to earn for itself a place of distinction. Nevertheless, the basic values that have endured in folk dance as art should be carried over into the subtler expressions of present-day art dance. The qualities of group feeling, simplicity, and seeming artlessness of execution should never be lost sight of. All these should be present in any dance and at all levels of artistic development; they may be sought and achieved in terms of what is organic to each level. The greatest heritage which folk dance has left us is the knowledge it gives of enduring art qualities inherent in the folk idiom.

At present there is a renewed interest in folk dancing. In many communities, and especially in cities that have a foreign population, there are groups that enjoy meeting to dance their own folk dances. To those who feel the need to identify themselves with their cultural past, and to others who join the dances to partake of their spirit and gaiety, such opportunities will afford a deep and pleasurable experience. Yet in the revival of these dances, especially of those which developed on foreign soil, the spirit of the dances cannot remain the same because the original motive is no longer present. In most instances the original motive was imitative magic, which has had to give way to the inventions of advancing civilization, causing the primal significance to weaken or disappear. It is the forms that remain to be enjoyed for the pleasure of their performance.

Although we may be accustomed to think of folk dances as rather simple, they have proven to be sources of inspiring material, rich in rhythmical intricacies which may be developed to a high level. Where there has been time and opportunity for some of these forms to undergo the normal process of change among the folk themselves, or where an artistic adaptation of them has been made, we find that they have naturally become dances of the ballroom. This is what we observed in the seventeenth century, when the dancing masters of that time intruded with their artistry and skillfully transformed the more vigorous forms of the folk into the polished aristocratic forms of the court. Many of these dances exist today and continue to delight us with their rhythm and grace.

The kinds of movements that are usually thought of as belonging to folk dance are movement experiences belonging to everyone. They are universally interesting and enjoyable because in them we find vigorous dance activity pleasurable for its own sake. However, when particular folk dances are used, they should be taught recreatively so that their spirit may be recaptured, as opposed to the deadly method of memorizing step sequences as a revival of the original forms. Our culture of the twentieth century is far from having a folk character, and it would be presumptuous to lay claim to the art experience of another culture by learning to copy its forms. But we may find pleasure dancing in the folk idiom, not because the dances are folk dances, but because they are based upon common experiences and employ a kind of dance activity available to all, and because we share in the underlying emotion of life and its universal type of activity.

Thus we see that this stage of dance experience is a grade not to be skipped while we advance to the more sophisticated, expressive forms of a maturing mind. It is dancing for fun; out of it will arise the need for a more serious study of dance as a conscious art form of expression.

Since the appeal of folk dances to the average American is largely pleasure in vigorous rhythmic movement, rather than in any wider orientation of imaginal experience, it seems a pity that children and older students are not led into the thrill of composing and dancing their own dances. Groups today, surely, are as capable of creative activity as were the peasants of another age.

Contemporary

The spirit of inquiry and science, which characterizes the twentieth century, is rooted in the awakening and development of preceding ages. There have been retreats and advances, failures and successes, civilizations constructing and achieving, nature destroying and revitalizing. Sometimes a social ideal has inspired a new doctrine; sometimes political or spiritual ideals have been the battleground in a struggle for larger rights. Always the successive ideals and achievements seemed the adequate expression of their time. The values of every age are a reflection not only of its own ways but of those in the age that preceded it. Consequently, no age can escape the obligation to pass on something of value to the next!

The last few centuries, and especially our own, have been spectacular in the progress of individual opportunity and in the advance of the natural sciences. In the nineteenth century these basic sciences were lifted from the realm of metaphysical abstractions and placed in the laboratory, from which they have emerged as exact sciences. New facts were discovered, new conclusions drawn, and new theories formed. From these arose new philosophies and a strong movement toward intellectual freedom. Man's outlook changed. He discovered himself. He believed in himself, and with this belief came a thirst for new knowledge as distinct from the renewed interest in ancient knowledge which marked the beginning of the Renaissance.

The present century has seen the miraculous results of a civilization devoting its energies to mechanical invention. This invention has given us great factories, mass production, capitalists, wage earners, unions, strikes, lowered cost of material goods, higher standards of living, swifter transportation, electricity, advertising, magazines, telephones, radios, airplanes, all expressive of a feverish eagerness for more abundant living.

Man's horizon is infinitely larger, but the abundant life is still a mirage. These so-called higher standards have not yet been sufficiently realized in the betterment of humanity or in the educational and artistic aspects of living.

Instead, we are overcommercial, overeager for riches. This is understandable. Our early days were spent in pioneering, in clearing forests, in acquiring homes, in establishing law and order, and in developing American principles of education and government—the first essentials. These first necessities demanded all that men had of stamina in body and spirit. The aesthetic nature was perforce neglected. Later came the days of boom and reckless extravagance of the era after the Civil War, ruthless in business and keen in politics. Great fortunes were amassed. There was little thought of or inclination to art, save with a few. Only money was held in esteem. In fact, men prided themselves on their lack of convention and on their contempt for the aesthetic. It was a low ebb in our cultural history. As in the pioneer days, the atmosphere was not conducive to an art that could be considered an expression of American life. Few writers or painters were produced in this time. Neither was the atmosphere favorable to the cultivation of that sympathetic understanding so necessary to the spiritual sustenance of artists. Art does not come to a people while they are struggling for material existence. And, likewise, the ease and irresponsibility of a too pampered life do not key to a pitch for vibrant expression. Rather they are apt to make flabby and nonresilient the sounding board of vital human responses.

One of the effects of this rough and ready existence, where men fought nature and competed with their fellows in business and politics, was to create an attitude of rugged individualism which is still prevalent.

Although we live in a land of great individual opportunity, we carry on a deadly conformity in the midst of our much-boasted freedom and individualism. We dress as others dress, we read the same books, we think the same thoughts, and we dance as others are dancing—afraid to be ourselves if to be ourselves means to be different. We fear what others might say. Although secure in individual freedom and opportunity, we are

A CULTURAL SURVEY OF DANCE

insecure within ourselves as individuals. We feel safe in conforming, in being like others. Psychologically we are not yet mature. Conformity, however, has always existed in human society and is a definite characteristic of primitive and folk culture, of young life, of adolescence, and of the immature adult mind. Even so, we must realize that slavish conformity reflects a dominance of the acquisitive instinct that takes over the creations of others with no effort to know or understand. It is the easy way, but it is an attitude that quells the spirit of inquiry and the impulse to create. The result is a rigid living that breeds distrust and intolerance of other ways of life.

To help our people mature and raise our cultural level, we must give them the same opportunity for artistic and spiritual growth that has been afforded them in other branches of education. The creative and artistic potentialities must be unleashed and cultivated if many songs are not to be left unsung.

If we are to understand contemporary dance better, we must keep an outline of pioneer conditions in mind. We must have also an understanding of the social, economic, scientific, and ideological conditions out of which dance is developing. A living art must be aware of the problems of its own age and discover answers in terms of that age. It cannot express feelings and ideals that have vanished or adopt techniques and aims without consideration of their pertinence. We must bear in mind that new problems confront us which demand solution.

It is always true that dance, whether robust and spontaneous, restrained and ceremonial, or stilted and formal, will be an expression of the age that produces it. Now, as in the past, dance reveals the spirit of its own age.

In many respects our dance resembles folk dance in its vitality and expressive values. But there are these differences. Today dance as a fine art employs technical skill to attain a perfect utterance, whereas folk dance employs its movements more unconsciously and spontaneously. Also, the attitude of the individual dancer is somewhat different. Unlike folk dance, which, as we have seen, is primarily a social and group activity, contemporary dance is both social and individual. The dancer today is free to interpret a wide range of experience and, as far as he is able, to reveal his visions through his own dance forms. He is free to dance his own style and to symbolize his own meanings. At the same time he feels that communication also is essential to his art and that its value depends upon its broad significance for others. He realizes that he is a social creature, a focus of drives and forces that are also acting upon his fellowmen. Thus in his dancing the universal is realized in the individual. As with the folk dancer, the art of the dancer today must be significant in meaning and communicative in movements if it likewise is to be of social value.

Until recently, the fortunes of dance in America have been relatively poor. Because of Puritan influence there was very little dancing in our earlier history, especially in the North. Later, through the more liberal settlements of the South, the square dances, the waltz, and the popular English folk dances entered.

For many years, however, especially since the introduction of jazz, there has been no popular form of dance that is in any sense artistic. Of course, there have been schools of dancing of one kind or another, but the number of people who could take advantage of these schools was necessarily limited.

Dance has, however, continued in a form that must not be underestimated—the social dance as we know it today. Unfortunately, these dances represent little of true art value and offer no real opportunity for entering into larger group feeling. In contemporary social dancing, the higher elements of dance seem to have vanished, leaving little that is artistic or gratifying as an aesthetic experience. It makes almost no claim to decorum, courtesy, charm, or dignity and grace of movement. This is a pity, for the ballroom is well suited to the social graces, which, though limited in appeal, are a source of delight to the aesthetic nature. Furthermore, novelty is overstressed in our couple dancing. Fashion's decree in one season may require an affectation of the grotesque or the exotic, in another the imitation of foreign forms. Although the impulses and motives that actuate our social dancing are of primary and fundamental origin, its forms belong to society and to the mode of the moment, and are too artificial and fleeting to last.

Under such conditions these sophisticated dance forms are bound to suffer from lack of inspiration and genuine artistic intention. But not all artistic value is lost to ballroom dancing. Although it is not the true nature of the social dance to exist as a fine art, there are many square and round dances that afford group pleasure, and for those who prefer couple dancing there is every opportunity to enjoy and develop skill and grace of movement. The results and the satisfactions depend entirely on the taste of the dancer, on what he expects to get from dance, and on what he desires to contribute to it. Within the last few years many fine artists have devoted their skill to raising ballroom dancing to a higher level. There may be too much social dancing, and much that is not good, but, if it can lift dull spirits, we should recognize at least that much value in it.

In the early years of the present century there was a movement in the United States toward a more satisfying type of dance than then existed. A reaction set in against the superficial and sterile forms of foreign importations, which had been the only ones available. Soon attempts were made to lead people back to the Greek ideal of dance, which was then thought to be movement founded on the law of natural motion and rhythm. This development began in private studios and gradually spread to colleges and public schools. The leaders of this movement went to the Greeks because they had accorded dance so high a place in the education of youth. From the Greeks the leaders learned again the educational value of dance and the need for a technique which rests upon fundamental, natural principles, and not upon unnatural body positions.

This concept of dance had a rapid and merited growth, but unfortunately too many were unprepared, both technically and imaginatively, to grasp its essential features. The very beauty of Greek art contributed to this result, for with the return to the

Greek ideal there was also a return to its themes, which so poetically and beautifully interpret the great force of life and reflect so profound an understanding of its meaning—but which, it appeared, could not be transplanted. Much of the dancing of this period lacked form and purpose and would seem sentimental to us today. Another difficulty was the attempt to dance the "Greek way," imitating its forms from Greek pictorial art, rather than to dance creatively under the inspiration of its ideal and with a real conviction of its meaning and significance. It was not sufficiently realized that, as the Greeks had danced the life of their times, so we should dance the life of ours.

Yet out of this movement has grown a broader and, we hope, a wiser one. It has been recognized that the great emotions which are the themes of so many dances are to be found in all ages, but that the manner of expressing them will differ from age to age.

Since the World War America has become aware of herself and consequently interesting to herself. As Americans we are changing our ideas of what makes life worth while and what constitutes success. This new America is a stimulating scene of activity for artists to interpret. They are finding her vastly interesting, and the public in turn is becoming interested in the artists' interpretations of and comments on its life and culture.

Perhaps more important than any other one cause of speeding up this new relationship between public and artist was the financial crash of 1932. The public's interest in its artists and concern for their welfare were evidenced by the government's com-

33

ing to their aid. First there was established in 1933 the Public Works Art Project, which was active for a few months only. Its purpose was relief. After it closed down, the Section of Fine Arts was established by the Treasury Department; its function was definitely not relief, but the employment of artists on the basis of the quality of their work.

The government's aid was not limited to architects, painters, and sculptors. It extended a helping hand to actors and dancers. Space will permit us only to mention the establishment of the Federal Theater Project, and to note in passing that in 1937, because of a curtailment of government funds, the Dance Unit of this project was dissolved. Even though the plan never materialized, it is gratifying to know that in the summer of 1939 the Section of Fine Arts was considering including dance in its program.

From such a general interest in art, it was to be expected, there would come a broadened interest in dance. At the present writing the United States is becoming increasingly dance-conscious. The impulse to dance is certainly more insistent with us than ever before. We have an army of young enthusiasts—students, dance groups, dance artists and teachers—who through their efforts in performance and teaching are influential in bringing forth a dance that is American—American in the sense that our dancers and student dancers are turning to the life they know for their material and are seeking their own appropriate forms of expressing them. To this developing interest a great impetus has been given during the last twenty years by the departments of physical education for women in our universities and colleges, whose farseeing directors had a vision for dance and included it as an important part of the physical education program. They have made it possible for thousands of students to enjoy dance as a pleasurable creative art experience, and in many instances talent has been released for later development and artistic careers.

Social centers and the Young Women's Christian Associations are more and more including dance instruction in their programs, all of which has stimulated dance interest and appreciation and aided definitely in the gradual acceptance of dance as an art. In fact, the time has come for its place in our educational program to be challenged. It is rightly being considered as belonging to the department of fine arts. But, unless the change of administration would continue to make it as accessible to students as it is in the departments of physical education, it is better for it to remain with the department of its adoption. Had it not been for the opportunity given dance by physical educators, it would have had little chance for growth in this country.

The number of universities, colleges, elementary schools, and high schools that are giving dance a place in their programs is large; yet, considering the number of schools in this country that offer no dance instruction of any kind, we can realize the extent of pioneer work yet to be done.

Another proof of a spreading interest in the educational possibilities of dance was manifested by the International Dance

DANCE: A CREATIVE ART EXPERIENCE

Conference held in Paris during the summer of 1937, for the single purpose of considering the educational values of dance. This was indeed encouraging, for the countries of Europe had not until then revealed an interest in the more general cultural values of dance.

Dance International 1900–1937, held for five months in New York City during the winter of 1937–1938, was a stimulating event to the dance-interested public. It was primarily interested in the cultural value of dance. To emphasize this, its program included exhibits of related art works, collected from all parts of the world, that had received their inspiration from dance; photographs; books on dance; motion pictures and talks; and dance programs organized to present, as far as possible, all the different forms of dance being done in the United States today. The many who witnessed the exhibits and programs must have been impressed with the development of dance, especially in this country since 1900.

But with all this dance interest and energy we have not yet a general public clamoring for it, or a farseeing theater management which realizes dance as a legitimate branch of the art of the theater. With government interest and subsidy, there was hope that a theater dance might evolve from the American scene—a theater dance that in every way would prove itself a serious and influential art in the cultural life of our communities. There are, however, a few theater managers who, believing in dance, have enthusiastically admitted dancers to their theaters

36

and usually at a financial loss. We may look at least to two sources for this difficulty: the lack of appreciation by audiences of the art of the dancers, and the failure of many of the exponents of contemporary art dance to communicate to their audiences. They have not yet presented dance in a form that is sufficiently intelligible and moving to our large lay audiences. Naturally, people will not become enthusiastic patrons of an art they cannot understand.

If the theater is to be one of the means through which dance is to reach the public, it must take upon itself a form and manner of presentation that is both expressive and communicative—yet without loss of artistic integrity. But it must be remembered that a very large proportion of dance audiences today is composed of those who think of dance only in terms of entertainment. They have not had the opportunity to study movement as a medium of expression. Therefore, the most advanced forms of art dance are likely to be meaningless to them. The motor symbols are strange to their movement experiences. Consequently, they are baffled because they have no contact with the experiences of the dancer. People go to the theater to partake of emotional experience, to have their concentration on everyday affairs broken down, and to be made to concentrate with the artists and live their experiences. One of the measures of an artist's greatness is his ability to do this with his audiences. It is very understandable how an artist desires to present those works that best represent his maturity. The situation could be greatly helped if our artists

DANCE: A CREATIVE ART EXPERIENCE

would devote part of their programs to dances that manifest their highest and most perfected creations, and so gradually develop audiences to a fuller appreciation of dance as a fine art.

To help meet the problem of developing an understanding laity, dance should be included as a part of the art education of children in our schools, for they are to become the future dance audience. Such a condition is essential before any art can become socially and culturally significant; and when dance reaches this status, it is but a step to its entrance into the theater. As dance becomes an accepted art of the theater, it will be in a vital position to exist as a force in the art world today and as a cultural influence in any thinking community.

The ballet is a form of theater dance that continues to be popular in the more urban centers of this country, although as an art form it has never taken deep root in American soil. Its earliest importations were taught by foreign dance masters, and in essence they were dances of an aristocratic Europe which had lost its spark. Being taught privately, ballet was a form only for the privileged few. But with the coming of the Russian ballet to America in 1914, it increased in popularity. Its glamorous setting and costumes, the superb technical attainment of its individual dancers, and its mass movement and music are isolated qualities of perfection to be admired. However, they are not qualities that completely satisfy the requirements of dance as a fine art. As a theater art, dance should inspire and thrill, and cause man to think and feel. If ballet were denied its spectacular settings, costumes, and orchestra, and were forced to rely upon its movements for conveyance of meaning, it is doubtful if it would carry much significance as drama or dance. Both the technique and the themes seem to have lost touch with life, with the common human impulses from which all the arts spring. The principles of movement in the conventional ballet are not concerned with the study of movement as a medium of expression. The traditional ballet is the victim of a technical system that has remained almost unaltered for two centuries, and its inadequacy for today is revealed by the futility of its effort at creative expression.

However, there is evidence that ballet, too, is in a state of transition. Out of all the great flux that dance is in today, there should arise a ballet rejuvenated by the new forces of contemporary dance, which offer a fuller technique and a greater range of dramatic expression than have been possible heretofore. To accomplish this will require a genius able to organize all the necessary phases of theater production and at the same time to direct in such a way that dance will remain a living and animated art.

But, despite the many encouraging signs, contemporary dance is beset by many problems. Because it has been for so long, and is so often, degraded and exploited, it still meets with indifference and opposition even in its highest forms. It is rejected on pseudo-moral grounds. The type of dance usually found in music halls and other places of entertainment contributes to this attitude. This condition, in part, is due to the overcommercialization of the whole theatrical profession and to the attitude of many impresarios. Their chief interest, too frequently, has been in commercial gain, rather than in any cultural philanthropic endeavor. As a result, the value of a dancer's art is often judged by box-office receipts. Such measures have caused the art as a whole to suffer.

And again, the endless variety of activities presented in the one name of dance has helped to confuse the layman's conception of dance, which for the most part is based upon his knowledge of ballroom, tap, and acrobatic dancing. And his conception of dance as a creative art is further confused by the many imitators of the individual artist dancers. Imitative dances become routine effects and as such have little to offer as art.

The status of dance is further complicated by many concurrent regional developments. Such local variations and particularized ideals are healthy if not carried too far, for each region must have its own cultural pattern to produce its particular dance. But no regional development should be made the criterion of the proper aesthetic forms in other areas. Each region should be free to follow and perfect its own expressive needs. Wherever there has been a tendency to elevate the ideas and themes of a particular locale into laws for the whole art, the results have been unfortunate.

Under these circumstances it is not surprising that dance, even of the highest type, meets with much misunderstanding. This condition would be much less serious if we had a well-developed national criticism in our country. The lack of it, and the fact that there is as yet no accepted philosophy or agreement as to the value of dance, are two of the most serious obstacles in the growth of dance today.*

There is a genuine need for a sympathetic and informed group of dance critics who would not only help to educate the public and clarify popular ideas of dance but also be a source of help to the dancer. Sensitive, impersonal evaluation in which both audience and artist would have confidence would unquestionably improve the quality of dance and eliminate some of its weaker characteristics. At the same time we are grateful for the few critics now in this field.

Transition

Dance today is clearly in an unsettled state. Old forms and traditions are being given up. New ones are arising to take their place. A time of change presents a confused picture. That there is this change is proof that dance is organically vital—and much more so than it has ever before been in this country. As in all times of transition, some will be set adrift, others will see clearly where they are going, and leaders will continue to arise, who, it is predictable, will become authoritative and dogmatic. But in this day of broader knowledge and understanding it should be possible to include in our instruction the valuable phases and ideas

* In the summer of 1937, the Dance Section of the National Association of Physical Education launched an extensive questionnaire study of dance in various sections throughout the United States. Its purpose was to see if there is, or could be, an agreement as to the larger values of dance, its philosophy, and the educational values that should be stressed in its instruction. The outcome of this study should be very pertinent to all dance instruction in this country.

of leaders and to break down that attitude of mind which not only causes distrust of all that is unfamiliar but creates an unfavorable atmosphere for the growth of an art.

The United States is dynamic and spirited. Until now no particular dance has come forth to express its constructive creativeness. We abound with exuberant youth. What art expression is more necessary to the expression of the forces and impulses of young life than dance! There is no more immediate art.

The modern way of viewing the world is analytical. Science reveals new truths which enable us to build up criteria for evaluating experience. As far as we know, people of earlier ages did not have the tools of analysis which are ours. The total experience had to suffice them. And, further, artists today have better opportunities of becoming more aware of the intricacies and complexities of their respective media. Through scientific study new truths are revealed. With understanding come greater power, new controls, new forms expressing new experiences. Is this not the demarcation which separates ancient art from modern?

To understand dance today it has been necessary to view the past in the light of successive reactions, observing the conditions that gave rise to racial, folk, and aristocratic dance forms, and those that led to their full growth and decline, appreciating at the same time the contributions these various forms have made to the development of dance as a more mature art. Its history is rich in interest and fact. This discussion, however, is in no way offered as a history, except in a very elementary way. It has been presented rather as a paragraphing of the past.

A CULTURAL SURVEY OF DANCE

We have observed that, as man lives longer and gains more experience and a better understanding of his world, his ability to adjust himself and survive depends more and more upon his mental powers rather than upon physical prowess alone. Along with the evolving intellectual life our aesthetic and emotional natures have developed, and with this complex scheme of development our sense of values and our tastes have grown. Therefore dance, as an art form, is a medium that has always reflected man's mental evolution. His artistic evaluations are reaching higher and higher, and in the process his aesthetic needs are preferring abstraction as suggestion, rather than realism as detailed description and copy. But the same life forces will actuate the dances of today as in the past. Man feels as deeply now as then. Feeling is constant. Only form is variable. What has happened is that racial and folk tendencies have gradually developed into more spiritual ideals, which are the motives for expression. Experience tends to universalize the individual to the extent that concrete emotions and concrete dramatic situations take on more abstract form in the art expression of them.

Thus during the march of the ages man's expressive movements have become modified by his growing realization of the effect of his own actions, until at last these actions have been consciously and intentionally used as expressive tools. It was when thus modified that expressive movement became art dance—a form consciously pursued for its art values.

The desire and need for communication as well as for expression have led man to the discovery of aesthetic means. From this

43

search for a means have evolved the knowledge, science, and technique of dance. At the same time this search has led to a refining of the basic impulses, causing various civilizations to elaborate and standardize forms of emotional expression. With dance, the result of this refinement has thwarted and almost obliterated the instinctive desire to express ourselves through movement—so much so that one of our main problems today is to revive, through some kind of movement education, the impulse to move expressively, to dance, to develop adequate techniques for artistic expression.

The technique of dance is profiting from increased knowledge of motion and rhythm as applied to the movements of man. Physiological and psychological research have revealed to us the nature of the kinesthetic sense, the kinesthetic basis of rhythmic perception, and the relation existing between feeling and its motor expression—revelations which have made possible a new technical training. Also, the present scientific attitude has encouraged a habit of mind that is reflected with great benefit in our dance forms. It has made for clarity, simplicity, and directness. Its honesty of thinking leads to genuineness of feeling, which leaves little chance for superficiality. Although the less forceful rhythms of nineteenth-century romanticism have been replaced by the more vigorous, pulsating, and varied rhythms of our less leisurely age, that does not mean that the romantic spirit and sentiment are lost to us of today. Their mode of expression has merely changed to the modern idiom—meaning the discarding of unnecessary embellishments in the effort to attain a direct and frank simplicity of movement. Only such a dance form could be the correlate of the wide-ranging, complex, intellectual, and cosmopolitan character of our age. Its direction as a fine art is toward universal symbolism, much broader in its scope and meaning than any racial art or the art of any one age.

We are not concerned with traditional values as answers to problems that no longer exist. We make use of the same primitive elements with which our ancestors began, but with a difference: once a reflex outlet for strong emotional pressure, dance has become deliberate creation in which the intellect and will dominate the automatic and emotional impulses. There is a gain in consciousness, but no change in the essential working of biological and aesthetic processes. There is merely a refining of their functioning. We no longer expect dance to be the expression only of the more lofty and poetic feelings, but accept it as the expression of all that the heart can feel—its pangs, ecstasies, passions, moods, and aspirations. Its manner may include the satiric, the lofty, the simple, and the extravagantly strange. Dance will continue to grow despite confusion concerning its meaning and the various forms of its utterance.

The pleasure of obeying the impulse to move and to express in ordered movement our responses to the forces of our nature and of our environment remains the same in every time and place. The differences between the dances of the past and those of the present are but differences in outer form: in period, location, temperament, education, and taste, which together determine the cultural values of any age. Basically concerned with the primary issues of life, dance has been inseparably connected with the expression of the cultural development of every period, and in turn has exerted its influence on the social patterns of the past. Likewise, it can serve us today in our quest for richer living.

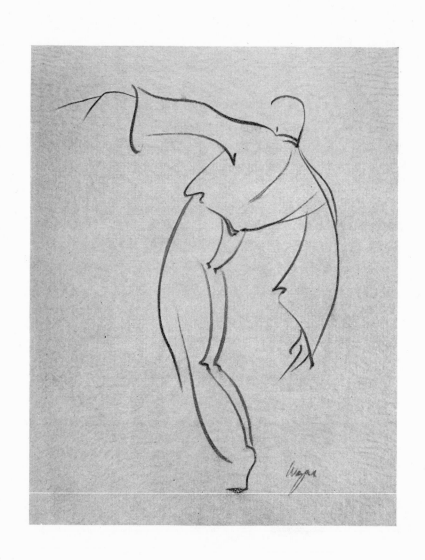

Chapter 2

THE PROVINCE OF DANCE

*Dance as an art, when understood,
is the province of every human
being.*

HAVING MADE certain claims for dance, we must justify them. To justify them we must consider the essential nature of dance as an art and the values of art in general.

To understand art fully and to appreciate the claims of dance as art, we must first appreciate the relations which have existed between man and his works—between the mind and its manifold expressions. The clarification of these relations will help us to understand the nature of dance as a separate art.

The story of art covers the whole sweep of human life. It has changed as man has changed. It varies with his religion, his philosophy, and his social relations. When man appeared on earth, he came with no fund of intellectual knowledge or experience behind him. He was born into a world not designed for his needs. He was forced to rely upon his instincts and what intelligence he possessed to bring about an adjustment with the world in which he found himself. Gradually, because of the action and interaction between the powers inherent in his nature and the forces of his environment, he developed into a better-adapted, more sensitive, more rational, more communicative self. He learned to live in his world and with his fellows.

In this slow process of civilization, art, an activity of man's own creation, has always been a significant influence. It has revealed a need that seems to be as fundamental as that of adaptation, a need that continually urges man to fashion his works as objects of beauty. It is when the spontaneous expressive efforts become modified by man's growing realization of their effect upon both himself and others, and are used consciously and

49

intentionally as expressive tools, that expressive acts become art.

Unfortunately, art is popularly thought of only in terms of its highest productions, as masterpieces existing in galleries; and artists, consequently, have come to be considered a special class who practice their art professionally. Such views have made the creation of art seem remote from the life of the everyday man, and art something that can be enjoyed only after years of study and close contact with genius. It is, of course, true that the greatest art can be created and fully appreciated only by the expert few; but it is just as true that a genuine appreciation and even true artistic creation are possible to all. One of the problems confronting teachers of art education is the danger involved in too high a degree of specialization. At the same time it is necessary to maintain a real appreciation of the efforts of those who are the greater artists.

Robert Henri makes a comforting statement for those not destined to be great in art when he says: "Art, when really understood, is the province of every human being. It is simply a question of doing anything well. It is not an outside, extra thing. When the artist is alive in any person, whatever his kind of mind may be, he becomes an inventive, searching, daring, self-expressive creature. He becomes interesting to other people. The world would stagnate without him—and the world would be beautiful with him. . . . He does not have to be a painter or a sculptor to be an artist. He can work in any medium. He simply has to find the gain in the work itself, not outside of it. Museums of art will not make a country an art country. But where there is the art spirit, there will be precious works to fill museums." *

Although art has been explained in many ways, it cannot, as Yrjö Hirn convincingly shows, be reduced to the play impulse, or the impulse to attract, or the impulse to imitate, though all these purposes, no doubt, have some influence in the development of art forms. Rather, the impelling force in art creation is to be explained by the psychology of feeling and by the need of communication. Every high-strung emotional state which has not found its appropriate expression causes movement by which we instinctively try to get rid of the feeling of restraint. As Hirn goes on to say, "art production would never have reached so high a development if it had served only as a sedative for human feelings. But neither does art, any more than the directed activities of expression, involve mere excitement; it too fulfills, and even with greater efficacy, a relieving and cathartic mission. While supplying man with the means of intensifying the feelings connected with all the varied activities of the soul, art at the same time bestows upon him that inward calm in which all strong emotions find relief. Every interpretation of art which does not pay due attention to both of these aspects must needs be one sided and incomplete." †

This desire to express all feeling in order to continue pleasur-

* Robert Henri, *The Art Spirit* (Philadelphia, J. B. Lippincott Company, 1923), page 5.

† Yrjö Hirn, *The Origins of Art* (New York, 1900), page 70, by permission of The Macmillan Company, publishers.

able states of feeling and to relieve those which are not pleasurable has its basis in the physiological phenomena of all life. Its foundation is analogous to that kind of response which causes the lowest forms of life, such as the amoeba, to move toward stimuli that are pleasant and to withdraw from stimuli that are unpleasant. All that we have at our disposal for human development is this natural and universal setup of simple feeling. Out of this, according to our disciplined tastes, we elaborate those superior feelings which later will serve us as our preferences.

Throughout our complex life, our habits depend on this physiological fact of reacting to pleasant and unpleasant stimuli. All movement, no matter how complex, is essentially built up within this instinctive expansion and contraction. It is instinctive to try to give external reality to our feelings in such a way as to bring others to partake of them. This transmission of feeling to others, and their response to one's own emotion, greatly enhance the original emotional state of the creator and are thus another source of pleasure in artistic effort. It was this desire to perpetuate his thoughts and feelings that led man in the first place to discover a way of translating them through whatever medium he had at hand, as well as he could within the limits of his powers of execution. This craving to have others feel as we do, to experience the enrichment of their response to our feeling, has led to artistic production. Man feels the need, but it is the artist in him that discovers the way of satisfying this need. For, back of all the various manifestations of art in all its stages, from that in which it was merely a crude, spontaneous reflex of strong feeling, to those forms that express man's highest emotional life, the one fundamental impulse continues to be the same; namely, the craving for expression and the sharing of the enhanced emotional state.

Of course, not everyone can be an artist in the more limited sense of the word. But, if we recognize that it is the nature of the original impulse that leads to creative activity, and the emotional value of its expression that distinguishes any activity as art, then we shall see that he who approaches his work in a creative spirit and makes it the expression of his own vision of life is an artist. To quote Hirn once more: "From the point of view of artistic perfection, there is all the world between the youthful verses of Goethe and the doggerel of a common schoolboy. But, psychologically, the schoolboy's doggerel may be the result of as strong a craving for poetic expression as any of the world's greatest poems. . . . If the notion of art is conceived in its most general sense, every normal man, at some time of his life at least, is an artist in aspiration, if not in capacity." *

Carleton Noyes carries the same thought a step further: "The impulse to expression is common to all, the difference is one of degree. And the message of art is for all, according as they are attuned to the response. Art is creation. For the artist it is creation by expression; for the appreciator it is creation by evocation. These two principles complete the cycle; abstractly and briefly they are the whole story of art. To be responsive to the needs of life and its emotional appeal is the first condition of artistic

* Yrjö Hirn, *op. cit.*, page 21, by permission of The Macmillan Company, publishers.

creation. By new combinations of material elements to bring emotion to expression in concrete, harmonious forms—themselves charged with emotion and communicating it—, is to fashion a work of art. To feel in material, whether in the forms of nature or in the works of art, a meaning for the spirit is the condition of appreciation." *

Art forms do not give directly; we get their meanings indirectly from the imagery of the creator who embodies the experience. The real pleasure and value of a work of art, such as a painting, a dance, or a symphony, lie not so much in what we actually see or hear as in how we react to all that we perceive. These reactions serve as experience to be exploited by ourselves. It is the associations which are aroused that determine the richness of living, for our feelings are attached to past experience, and an observer can create only out of what he has already actually gone through or imagined. So, greatness in art is dependent not only upon the personal power and richness of the creating artist but also upon the richness of experience being communicated. We find satisfaction and beauty in the thing created in such proportion as we are able to react to it, and this will be measured by the presence of like qualities in our own conception of the created work. Real appreciation always implies a consciousness of ourselves in relation to the object.

The only true way of appreciating works of art is by becoming familiar with the conditions and causes which produced them.

* Carleton E. Noyes, *The Gate of Appreciation* (Boston, Houghton Mifflin Company, 1907), page 21.

THE PROVINCE OF DANCE

As we already know, in any art experience, whether one of creation or one of appreciation, the causes that generate the emotive impulses are the issues of life and their meanings as we have remembered them. We are the sum total of our experiences, and we can respond to things only in terms of what we are.

At the same time man needs to realize his dream of life in some form outside himself. This necessity is one of the most important of all the keys to his history. We may observe its working in all that he does—in speech, in dress, in manner, and, in fact, in all his inventions. As he reaches higher planes of thought, this desire for expression demands, of course, more appropriate means. Thus, from the beginning, there gradually evolved what are termed the fine arts: * dance, music, poetry, drama, painting, and sculpture. The various arts differ in their outward form, but they all have a common source in the fundamental human need of revealing the inner life in an external pattern.

In speaking of art, we must not let the particular kind of activity that produces artistic results become divorced from our everyday, common actions and experiences. Out of the disappointments, joys, sympathies, and sorrows of actual daily life,

---

* By *fine art* is meant art that is created for the sole purpose of satisfying man's yearning for the beautiful, rather than for the sake of utility. However, works created with a utilitarian need in mind may also satisfy the aesthetic craving of their designers. The point is that their purpose is not aesthetic alone. It is this singleness of purpose that distinguishes the fine arts from the many other art forms. Although the fine arts may not exist to meet utilitarian needs as such, they are purposeful in another sense—they satisfy the needs of the creative spiritual nature. By being able to distinguish between the various art forms in terms of their purpose, we realize their common ground and their claim to the title of art.

we build a world of desire; we think of things as we wish they might be or ought to be; we idealize, and art affords us the opportunity of actually experiencing these ideals.

In this way, all the arts are one—the expression of man's emotional experience, transformed by thought and intentionally given form in some medium perceptible to the mind. But each art, because of limitations and demands imposed by the laws of its particular medium, has its own peculiar province and its own way of fashioning its forms. Psychology teaches us that all mental activity tends to express itself in muscular and glandular activity. Every thought or impression from the external world entering consciousness by way of the senses must find itself an outlet over the motor-nerve paths to the muscles. Thus it is that we find mere random movements the most immediate release of simple feeling. Such movements, however expressive, cannot be considered dance as a consciously directed art expression; they are merely reflex accompaniment of feeling. For the same reason we do not say that a joyous running and leaping against the wind is art; it is expressive, but it is not expression as art. However, if we take the leaps and runs and the various reactions to the *feel* of the wind, and mold them according to the principles of artistic composition, we at once achieve art. It is the systematizing, according to the laws of a medium, that separates art from accident and nature. It is only when these random yet expressive movements are subjected to the harmonizing influence of rhythm, and consciously given form, that dance comes into being as an art form.

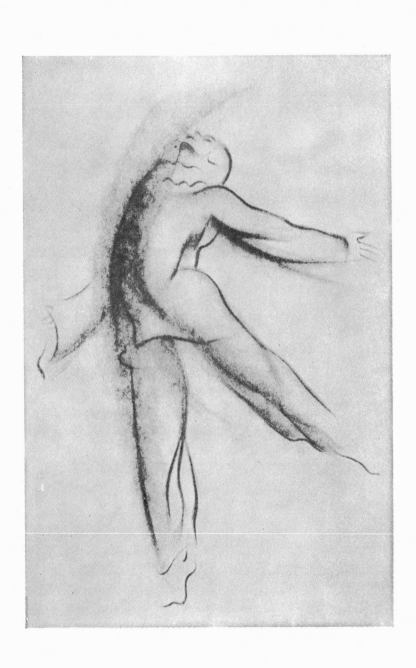

Chapter 3

EDUCATION THROUGH DANCE

No real intellectual, emotional, or artistic growth can take place save as it is built upon a foundation of innate capacities and impulses.

IF DANCE is to function again as a vital experience in the lives of our people, it must be the responsibility of our educators. The inclusion of dance in the general education program is the one means of giving free opportunity to every child for experiencing the contributions it can make to his developing personality and his growing artistic nature.

In considering such a plan we should be able to answer such questions as these: What do we mean by dance? What are its ultimate values and justifications? Of what importance is creative art activity in the development of the mind? And, finally, what is its value for the individual? Such a search into the nature of dance yields a philosophy based on a fundamental belief in the artistic and aesthetic capacities of human nature and in the values of expression through some creative art activity. From this philosophy must be formed a theory that will be an expression of the aims for which dance should work as well as a formulation of the underlying principles. An example of such a formulation is the insistence that dance be experienced as an adequate means of expression, so that, when the movements of the intellectual, emotional, and spiritual natures are co-ordinated with the activities of the body, there will result an expression that is vital and dynamic.

To work toward this end we must build a theory on a knowledge of the structure of the body and the laws of bodily movement. And to appreciate and understand the relation between feeling and action we must know the psychology of the emotions and the part they play in the urge to expression in movement. This carries us over into the science of dance: the systematized knowledge that tells us how to go to work—how to adjust our efforts to attain the desired ends. These ends will depend upon the view we hold for art, its social and individual values. Also, we must develop a technique that will result in forms that are in accordance with this artistic intention.

Education should be a building toward the integration of human capacities and powers resulting in well-adjusted, useful, balanced individuals. The desire to find peace within ourselves and to bring about an adequate adjustment to the life around us is the basis for all mental and physical activity. From birth to death life is a series of changing behavior patterns because life itself is an unfolding process. Just as the growth of man in civilization is the growth of man in consciousness, so is the educated, cultured, individual life dependent upon the growth and function of the mind, upon its capacity to know, will, imagine, create, and execute.

Everywhere educators are realizing that what is needed more than pedagogical preaching is intelligent stimulation to self-activity. There are, and always will be, many different theories of education. Often the education defined as "a preparation for life" has been so interpreted as to make it no more than a means of bettering one's economic condition. On the other hand, some critics seem to feel that the aim of education is success in living —quite a different matter. For this reason some thinkers and writers, especially those not in intimate touch with the actualities of education, have questioned the importance of creative activity and give but little place to the appreciation of beauty or the cultivation of artistic values. The reply to such attacks lies in a knowledge of the nature of the arts and in recent advances in educational theory.

No one who understands the relation of the arts to human personality can question their values in education, nor can those who have followed educational science during recent years fail to see that provision for the arts must be made in any adequate educational plan. If we go to one of the first masters of educational theory, Plato, we are told that "the purpose of education is to give to the body and soul all the beauty and all the perfection of which they are capable." This definition of purpose still holds, but today we would qualify Plato's statement in some such manner as that suggested by Spencer in his definition of life as "the conscious adjustment of internal relations to external." Both views, it is clear, focus upon the development and growth of the individual, and both imply self-activity, which we may take as the keynote of current educational speculation. The higher aim of education today is the development to the fullest extent of the growth of the individual, based upon a scientific understanding of all his needs and capacities. In so doing we try to attune our own thinking to harmonize with the student's particular interests because we realize that in his interests lies the key to his needs and capacities. Education cannot supply individual capacities—these must be inborn; but it can stimulate and aid in their growth; it can educate the student by giving him the opportunity to develop himself.

There are two aspects to education: one, the capacity to take in, to become impressed; the other, the capacity to give out, to express. To receive impressions informs the mind, but to express its reactions to these impressions requires co-ordination and co-operation of all the mental powers. Power to perceive and to evaluate experience is a high faculty, but of little use unless put into execution. Mere perception and comprehension of knowledge are not sufficient for the fullest development of the mind. To know is the essential first step, but it is the expression of what we know that develops character and a sense of values. It is through perception, intuition, feeling, and conception that our personalities assimilate experience and work it up into our own substance and the world of thought, emotion, and will.

Without this metabolism of experience damage is done to the emerging personality. It is likely to become overburdened and disorganized with undigested and unassimilated information, and inner spontaneity becomes hampered. If dance education is to contribute to this psychic integration, it is essential that the student experience movement in forms characteristic of human responses; that he be led, consciously, from the more natural movement types determined by structure to those responses that are variable and individually modifiable and under the control of higher associative processes; and, finally, it is essential that he experience and evaluate, as he progresses, the accompanying feeling tones of emotional enrichment.

In other words, dance education must be emotional, intellectual, and spiritual, as well as physical, if dance is to contribute to the larger aims of education—the developing of personality through conscious experiencing. It should capitalize every possible resource, selecting and integrating the contributions into a totality.

If we accept the belief in the organic wholeness of man, it is evident that the development of his energies must be interdependent. Our emotions and desires need intelligent selection and guidance, and to be carried to their fullest expression they demand skillful execution.

In such a concept of human development the body should be considered as the outer aspect of personality, for it is the agent through which we receive impressions from the external world and by which we communicate our meaning. Thus the body should be given as careful a study and as high a perfection of technique as the associated processes of thought and feeling. The most completely developed person is the one who has trained all his powers with equal dignity and consideration, in order that he may be physically, intellectually, and emotionally integrated. We may restate the meaning of education as the disciplining and training of our powers and the attainment of skill in execution.

The very nature of the arts makes them especially adapted to this ideal of education, for it is only in art that all the aspects of man's complex nature are united in expression. In art, as in reality, the drives are of the emotional nature; when subjected to the restraint and directions of the intellect and executed by the physical, they result in a fusion of all our energies with the focal point centered in the personality.

The place of dance in developing such individual growth is

DANCE: A CREATIVE ART EXPERIENCE

understood if personality is defined as the expressive total of all our physical, emotional, intellectual, and spiritual energies. These energies are in a constant state of reacting to and being acted upon by the social order in which we live. Of all the arts, dance is peculiarly suited to such a fulfillment of the personality. It serves all the ends of individual growth; it helps to develop the body; it stimulates the imagination and challenges the intellect; it helps to cultivate an appreciation for beauty; and it deepens and refines the emotional nature.

In the teaching and studying of dance we should not be concerned whether or not students develop into professional or recital dancers. The concern should be to develop the power of expression through the study of dance. It may be asked whether the expression of ordinary people has any particular value. It is true that expression is of special interest in professional art. We go to the works of the greatest artists for the wisdom and beauty and emotion they can communicate to us. But expression, execution, and sharing also belong to general education, and they are needs felt by all normal people.

Too often the tendency is to center dance education in performance, with the emphasis on technical skill, instead of studying the subject as a whole and using creative motor experience as the basis of instruction. In considering dance as an educational and creative art experience and not as performance, we should take care that students know dance as a special way of re-experiencing aesthetic values discovered in reality. Everyone has within himself the same potentialities as the artist dancer, but perhaps to a lesser degree. Everyone has intellect, emotion, spirit, imagination, ability to move, and educable responses. Every normal person is equipped with power to think, feel, will, and act. Anyone can dance within the limits of his capacities. To bring this to the realization of our youth necessitates an approach that is based on these fundamental human capacities. One of our problems is how to keep the creative impulse alive through the maturing years and how to help carry this impulse over into the realities of adult life with heightened power and more enlightened purpose. The basic forces underlying all living forms must be realized as the source of the creative impulse which impels to expression.

If dance is to realize these educational possibilities, it must take upon itself a form that is suited to them. It should base its movement forms on the laws of bodily motion, and the study of motion should include movement in all the forms characteristic of human responses. At the same time its techniques should be simple enough to afford the amateur student sufficient mastery of the body as his instrument of expression, and complex enough to prove interesting and valuable to those who wish to make dance their chosen profession. The rhythmic scope of dance will need to be sufficiently broad to include the varying personal rhythms of the students, and its forms and content will need to be flexible enough to provide opportunity for widely different expressions of widely different individuals.

Although such an approach to dance does not insist on artistic perfection from the professional critic's point of view, it can insist on high amateur standards and, in so doing, build a foundation for the development of a keen artistic integrity and appreciation. From such a background of study will arise those who are destined by original endowment to become our artist dancers. Our first concern is to teach boys and girls and men and women by means of dance, to teach dance as an experience that contributes to a philosophy and scheme of living.

It is to be expected that not everyone will be a great dancer, and that dancing, of course, will be experienced as a complete art form more by some than by others; but, as every child has a right to a box of crayons and some instruction in the fundamental principles of drawing and in the use of color, whether or not there is any chance of his becoming a professional artist, so every child has a right to know how to achieve control of his body in order that he may use it to the limit of his ability for the expression of his own reactions to life. Even if he can never carry his efforts far enough to realize dance in its highest forms, he may experience the sheer joy of the rhythmic sense of free, controlled, and expressive movement, and through this know an addition to life to which every human being is entitled. If the interest in giving instruction in dance is to produce dancers only, dance as a creative and pleasurable art experience, possible to all, is doomed.

It is because of this tendency that those who are convinced of the value of dance are striving to restore to society a dance that is creative, expressive, communicable, and social, a dance form that in every way will qualify as art.

Chapter 4
TECHNIQUE AND EXPRESSION

*Technique transforms experience
into the form of its expression.*

CIVILIZATION is the state of man. Man of all creatures is destined by the laws of his very nature to scale the heights according to his capacities for vision. His life is spent in seeking relations to the outside world. Living—being, adapting, becoming—is a process wherein man's inherent forces meet effectively the challenging forces of the outside world. Living becomes a series of conflicts in man's striving toward a goal. But there is conflict not only between man and his world, but within man himself—between the instinctive demands of the various powers of his complex nature. How much simpler human life would be if man's relations to his world and himself were like those in the plant or animal order, where relations are fixed and realized by an instinctive functioning of the creature's nature! But the solution of man's problems calls for powers of a higher order, demanding knowledge of himself. He must understand and know himself as an animal, as a man, as an individual, as an artist, and as a member of society. His primary nature will be understood as the plane where instinctive impulses operate. These impulses are powerful tendencies to action; they are the springs of future conduct. They are forces that need to be trained to serve the will and desires of an intellect impelled by ideals, so that man can bring all his powers to bear upon the life of his choice. Finding peace within ourselves and bringing about an adequate adjustment to the life around us are the bases of all mental and physical activity. All living is a process of solving problems as we become aware of them. Problem-solving is the basis of creative activity and is essential to all walks of life—work, play, and art.

DANCE: A CREATIVE ART EXPERIENCE

Any work of art begins with a purpose and grows through technique. In dance, as in every art, it is essential to train the mind to use some tool as an instrument with which to mold a medium into an art form.

In dance the body is employed as the instrument, and movement as the medium. Consequently, a dancer has two goals to keep in view. First, he must train the mind to use the body and to reflect its conditions, for the primary concern of dance is the feeling tones of physical origin. Second, he must train the body to be responsive to the expressive mind. Whatever thought and feeling tones are to be expressed must be felt through the body. Therefore the importance of feelings and emotions, and their power to motivate muscle activity, cannot be overlooked. Muscles contract in proportion to the intensity of the emotional drive of the experience to be expressed. This inner force, or motive power that drives us on in the life of our choosing, resides in that complex center which perceives, thinks, reasons, comprehends, remembers, imagines, and creates—the center we call mind.

Mind and Expression

Contemporary education regards the individual as a growing, changing organism whose mind becomes increasingly his most distinctive and dominant characteristic.

The word *mind* * is an abstract term. Every mind is a unique organization of impressions, intuitions, and beliefs which inter-

* A term here used for convenience to designate the mental aspect of the total organism, and not to imply a separation of mind from body.

prets all experience. The reactions of one mind will be different from those of a mind that has differently organized impressions. Every sensed impression takes its particular direction. Either it is arrested by counterimpressions, or it blends with past impressions and forms a definite feeling or attitude. Power of mind may be said to be the degree of strength of the stimulative and regulative processes which follow upon the perception of a stimulus. Therefore, experiences that have not been sufficiently perceived will contribute little or nothing toward expression. What has not impressed cannot be expressed. A properly functioning mind is constantly receiving impressions, associating them, refining them, selecting and releasing them, and so transforming them that they may better serve its purpose. The process whereby man gathers unto himself experience and performs acts manifesting sensation, choice, and volition, is accomplished through the nervous system by means of its stimulus-response mechanism. To achieve these integrated responses it employs special tools.

First of all there are those sense organs, or receiving organs (receptors), that pick up information from the outside world. They are terminal sensory structures adapted to receive various forms of environmental stimuli and to transmit them to the brain in the form of nerve impulses. Because of them we are able to "tune in" on all life's activities around us. These receptors are the only media through which the forces of the world outside or the generating forces within the body can reach the central nervous system and bring it into activity. They are the only way such forces can attain awareness. In this sense, the receptors may be thought of as analyzers of our environment, splitting it up into its component parts, each particular receptor attuned to certain aspects of the external environment and the *milieu intérieur*. Besides the usually mentioned five senses, there are organs of other senses—responsive only to conditions within the body itself. The group of sense organs that are of special interest in the study of movement are those in the muscles, joints, and tendons. They are stimulated by the activity of these parts, reporting to the mind the exact state of muscular contraction, the range of joint movement, and the tensions of the tendons in any movement. It is by means of this movement sense—the kinesthetic sense—that we can judge the timing, force, and extent of our movements, and adjust ourselves consciously or automatically to this information. To this group of receptors also belong the organs of static and equilibratory sensations, which serve to maintain body balance and posture.

The receptors, then, bring, as grist to the mill, a great mass of sensory material. The task of executing a reaction to this sensory material belongs to the effectors, which are the organs of response. Just as the receptors are specialized agents receiving stimuli, the effectors are specialized discharging agents. Between these lies a conducting tissue, serving an associative function as well as carrying impulses in and out. It also provides infinite possibilities for correlative action. With such an arrangement for association and overlapping of impulses, we can at once appreciate how infinite and vast are the possibilities of the mind, and can theorize that there are perceptual areas of the brain awaiting further sensitization to forms of energy pervading the ether, of which, as yet, man remains unaware.

Before an effective motor response is made, the great mass of incoming material undergoes a profound change. It becomes organized into definite ideas about, or images of, the environment upon which energy is expended. This change takes place in the cerebral cortex, where residues of past impressions are retained and where selective correlations and associations of great complexity take place. There emerge new behavior patterns in thought as well as in action. As the incoming impulses course toward the discriminating and organizing centers of the cortex, they are first delayed at a subcortical relay station, the thalamus. The reflex activity of the thalamus does not attain distinct consciousness, but nevertheless it contributes a feeling tone to the awareness ultimately aroused. The thalamus is often spoken of as the "old brain." It is important in lower forms without a cortex, and in man it retains its primitive functions. It is because of this contribution of the "old brain" that stimulation is directly connected with feeling tones, but it is the associative influences of the cortex that contribute toward enhancing their active manifestations. The cortex has a controlling or inhibiting influence over all the lower centers. If the path from the thalamus to the cortex is cut, there results excessive response to affective stimuli. There is an overloading of sensation with feeling tone because the regulating influence of the cortex has been released. This type of behavior is normally that of the immature mind, whether in a child, in primitive man, or in an immature adult. It seems that within this "old brain" resides the stored-up wisdom of the race—residues of racial experience that have helped man to survive and that are, therefore, rich in emotional tone. Indeed, the affective phase of sensations and the emotional life in general are believed to reside in this "old brain" and not in the cerebral cortex. The sensations, however, are without clear localization and discrimination. These need the co-operation of the cortex. The thalamus and the spinal cord take care of all impulses of the instinctive type without reference to the cortex, but they are not free of its inhibiting influence.

Another subcortical area that has profound influence upon all movement is the cerebellum. It does not initiate movement, but in some way it affects the tonicity of the muscles, for it has the power to augment the tonus of some muscles and diminish the tonus of the antagonistic muscles. It maintains proper balance of muscular contractions. The details of its functional activity, although appreciated, are not clearly understood. But it is certain that the cerebellum is the mechanism of unconscious motor co-ordination and is devoted chiefly to reflex and instinctive activities. Medical science has discovered that loss of tonicity, due to the impaired functioning of the cerebellum, results in increased mobility of the joints.

Intelligence and consciousness (the psyche) are believed to reside within the gray matter of the cerebrum. Correlations and associations of great complexity take place within it. It also possesses the ability to retain past impressions. It is so constructed that every part not only receives incoming impulses but originates outgoing impulses as well. Impulses that involve association, selection, and discrimination are referred to the cortex for these processes before being passed on to the effectors for execution. Thus it is evident that the co-operation of these higher and lower parts is essential for rich emotional experience, integration, and satisfying artistic expression through dance.

Although we are impressed with the complexity of the nervous system, its functioning principle is simple. But the true nature of the nerve impulse whereby out of experience man progresses to an ideal remains a mystery. When science can tell us what the nerve impulse is, then we can understand how learning takes place. Until then we can only avail ourselves of the facts known to date and build as firmly and wisely as possible a philosophy, a theory, and a science of our subject.

Such knowledge gives us security in believing in the educational significance of the capacity for individuality, in the ability and value of learning through conscious experience, and in the artistic necessity to create from consciously evaluated experience.

As to the educational significance of the capacity for individuality in development and the ability to profit by experience, C. Judson Herrick says: "So well have we learned the lesson that children bring with them into the world no mental endowments ready-made—no knowledge, no ideas, nor morals—but that these have to be developed anew in each generation under the guiding hand of education, that we devote one-third of the expected span of life of our most promising youth to the educational training necessary to ensure the highest possible development of the latent cultural capacities of these associational mechanisms of the cerebral cortex.

"But we have often been blind to the other side of the picture. We have seen above that the adult cortex cannot function save through the reflex machinery of the brain stem, and it must not be forgotten in our pedagogy that this relation holds in much more vital and significant sense in the formative years of the child. It is true that the child is born with no mental endowments; but how rich is his inheritance in other respects! He has an immense capital of preformed and innate ability which takes the form of physiological vigor and instinctive and impulsive actions, performed for the most part automatically and unconsciously. This so-called lower or animal nature is ever present with us. In infancy it is dominant; childhood is a period of storm and stress, seeking an equilibrium between the stereotyped but powerful impulsive forces and the controls of the nascent intellectual and moral nature; and in mature years one's value in his social community life is measured by the resultant outcome of this great struggle in childhood and adolescence. This struggle is education." *

If dance education is to afford an opportunity for the type of integrated experience mentioned in the preceding paragraph, which is essential to art, the student must experience movement in the various forms characteristic of human responses. He should be led consciously from the invariable type of actions that are pre-

---

* C. Judson Herrick, *An Introduction to Neurology* (Philadelphia, W. B. Saunders Company, 1931), page 374.

determined by his structural and reflex organization to those responses that are individually modifiable. These variable and personal responses are under the conscious selective control of the thinking, knowing self. As he progresses, he will be able to experience and evaluate the accompanying feeling tones which are the contribution of the emotional nature.

Movement and Expression

Expression and its forms are necessarily infinite, because of the many ways of experiencing, and, considering the great variety and range of movement of which the body is capable, we realize how complex the technical preparation for dance may be. Yet in this confused mass of material there are certain facts and principles upon which art results may be founded. The solution is to find these principles, to obey them, to admit their normality, and to perfect movement in accordance with them before submitting movement to the fashioning of the expressive mind.

Although movement sensations are important to all life activities, with most people they escape recognition. This is because muscular sensations are too indefinite to force themselves sufficiently upon the attention. Even when we are deprived of them, the defect is realized mainly in the loss of control rather than in a cessation of particular muscular sensations.

Ordinarily we look at movement superficially, noting only the results. We usually are not aware that actual muscles are involved —but rather pay attention to the external changes brought about by their action. In accordance with their results, actions are termed purposeful, impulsive, intelligent, expressive, artistic, and so on. But such terms do not suggest the intrinsic attributes of motion itself. The student of dance must go deeper. He must learn to be aware of muscular tensions, to discover in movement the manifestation of physical laws, and consciously to employ those laws if he is to develop a style in accordance with them.

A study of movement must penetrate into the *anatomical* factors of joint structure, which determine the range and kinds of movement (such as bending, stretching, and twisting), the various types of locomotion, and the load-bearing capacities. It is this anatomical structure that sets the mechanical limits for motor response.

But this structure, when it is set in action, is dependent upon *physiological* aspects. In the last analysis, movements that follow any stimulating cause are the manifestations of physiological principles. These principles in turn are attendant upon neural events. These physiological aspects pertain to the condition and nature of muscle tissue, which depends upon the nervous tissue for the impulse to set off its latent motor energy. They are the factors upon which the human mechanism is dependent and in accordance with which it must function. This neuromuscular setup is a behavior equipment possessing reflex paths and infinite possibilities of activity, which, when modified, emerge as definite skills. It is educated by doing.

But we are also designed to think and feel and will. The mere mechanical factors cannot explain the play of life. Therefore, we cannot submit to mechanical laws alone. Psychological factors also must be considered. These act not only through the will and association, but through the awareness of kinesthetic sensations and various mental states. To execute any movement, we must make an effort; this effort consists of an expenditure of energy. Subjectively it manifests itself by specific kinesthetic sensations —and the resulting mental state of ease or lack of ease plays an important role in determining the forms of our movements. Generally speaking, the movements that are most pleasurable are those that give us the greatest return for the most economical expenditure of energy, and not necessarily those which demand the least effort. This is important in the learning of new skills and in the satisfaction or dissatisfaction derived from them. Students are likely to become discouraged during the first unfruitful efforts, but, with an understanding of these conditioning factors, they will work with less discouragement and push on with enthusiasm to perfected forms. The mental equipment determines, then, the psychic behavior, for in it resides the awareness of all sensations as well as the capacity to think, feel, imagine, and will. It is the equipment for interpreting experience and represents the human personal endowments. It is the formative substance from which develops personality.

Further consideration of movement reveals an interrelation of various other factors that contribute to and condition its forms. Whenever movement of the body or its parts takes place, we observe that there is a change of position; that is, the body may change its position by moving from one place to another, or the parts of the body may change their positions with respect to one another and thus produce a postural change of the body as a whole. And, further, these changes may take place on a moving or on a stationary base. Change of position implies that *direction* is taken and *distance* is covered. Movement has *range*. Also, in covering distance, we consume *time*, which further implies *rate* of movement or execution. And, finally, for movement to be accomplished at all, *energy* must be expended with some degree of force. Also there must be a point of its application. No movement, however large or small, fast or slow, strong or weak, can take place unless resistance, direction, distance, duration, speed, and force are involved. A study of motion necessarily involves the consideration of these factors and the relation they bear one to another. Once the possibilities of combining these factors are understood, there is no end to the movement patterns and forms that the creative teacher or student may evolve as a means of stimulating and experiencing new motor responses.

For example, let us take locomotion as one of the ways in which the body may change its position in space. Locomotion is simply the transferring of the body weight from one foot to the other, or to both feet, or from both to both as in jumping. The varying ways in which the body structure permits this transference are commonly called walk, run, hop, leap, jump, skip, gallop, and slide. These are the untaught ways of locomotion due to the structural functioning of our body mechanism, and, no matter how complex a dance step may be, it will be found to be an organization of these elemental steps.

TECHNIQUE AND EXPRESSION

Qualities of Movement

Since energy is a determining factor in the character and expressiveness of movement, it is interesting to consider actions with respect to the way energy is released to produce them. For the sake of discussion we shall divide movements into four classes: swinging, percussive, sustained, and collapsing.

Swinging, or swaying, movements are characterized by a rhythmical to-and-fro action. They have a passive acceleration and retardation, as experienced when one swings in a swing. The return phase, or effort, is not made until the momentum of the preceding one has ceased. For this reason little fatigue accompanies such movements. Their effect is very soothing, and they easily establish themselves in a "one-two-three" rhythm, which has the power to stimulate repetition to an almost hypnotic degree. The rhythmical to-and-fro character of the typical swinging movement is easily changed to a to-and-fro movement of *pistonlike* character, if the moving part, such as an arm, is thrust forward and pulled back before momentum is overcome. Such movements are strenuous, stimulating, and fatiguing, because of the energy necessary to check momentum and to change direction.

Contrasted with the swaying movements are the jerky *percussive* movements. They are due to a sudden explosive release of energy, as in the alert, quick movement reactions when one is startled, or the protective actions of dodging, or a sudden thrust, as a punch. The percussive quality is present in acts of pushing, throwing, and striking, but in combination with other qualities.

81

It occurs at the particular phase within the movement phrase that will impart the most strength and speed to the object being moved, thrown, or struck. Jumping, leaping, running, and walking also have a percussive release but to a varying degree according to the activity. The preparatory movements of these actions are swinging or sustained, or may be a combination of both, and they are usually completed with a "follow-through" of action. If a series of short percussive movements proceed at a very rapid rate, their quality is changed to a vibratory effect.

Sustained movements are those that are executed with an even, steady energy release throughout the movement phrase, as in a steady pull, in slow, cautious movements, and in actions of balance. Sustained movements should be distinguished from the momentary suspension which, by an equalization of muscle tensions, occurs at the end of a swinging movement or at the end of the "follow-through" of a throw or a golf stroke. Or movement may be checked before action is completed, and the moving part, or the whole body, may be supported in suspension, seemingly without effort. It is the completion of the movement that gives the impression of suspension. Such actions have some percussive release of energy and in most instances are more easily arrived at from a swinging start.

Living and moving as we do in a gravitational field, gravity is a force that constantly exerts an influence on our actions. We are not so conscious of it until there is a complete loss of control, which means giving up to gravity; and the action is characterized by a *collapsing* quality. Such a release of energy may occur instantaneously throughout the whole body, resulting in a collapsing fall, as in fainting; or only a single part or several parts may be so released. When one falls, however, the movement may involve some resistance at the start and then end in a sudden collapsing release; or it may offer some resistance throughout the falling movement, in which case there would be very little or no collapsing quality.

Any continued physical action will include several of these qualities, and more than one may be present in the same motor act. It is only as one or the other dominates that an action is said to be of a certain type, such as percussive, sustained, swinging, or flowing. It is from the combination of these qualities, varied in direction, speed, distance, intensity, space relationships, and force, that a dance vocabulary may be discovered and built. By changing the dynamics of an action we change the *feel*. Therefore every movement has a feeling peculiar to it, and is a source of expression for later artistic intention.

Tension and Technique

Another important factor to recognize is that the skeletal muscles are in a constant state of activity or tension. They support the body against gravity, not only when it is in action, but when it is sitting or standing still. Therefore a constant flow of energy is maintaining balance between the parts of the body. This balancing of tension between opposing muscles results in muscle tone—an elastic tension which is inherent in our organic structure and is the basis of technique for expressive movement. All great dancers have this movement quality to a high degree. Although it is in part reflexly controlled, it can be further developed and controlled through conscious motor training and effort. This elastic tension is greatly reduced by fatigue and relaxation as well as by rigidity, which checks it. We relax to release, and we tense to support and to sustain. Progress in dance depends upon the development and control of this tension. It is only through proper tension that the muscles can adjust themselves to any desired intensity of energy release, to speed of execution, or to shades of artistic meaning. Furthermore, tension is essential to perfect coordination and heightens kinesthetic sensation, stimulating the mind to a keener motor awareness. The very basis for aesthetic experience in movement is this heightened sensitivity and awareness. When one is dancing, it must never for a moment be lost. All types of movement depend upon it. A flowing or sustained quality is quite impossible without it; quick, jerky, and vigorous percussive movements depend upon it and are unconvincing when they lack it. The more tensile the movement, the deeper the source of physical power. Ability constantly to readjust the balance between motor energy and emotional demands is technique.

Rhythm and Expression

The tendency to repetition is also inherent in muscle and nerve tissue. This persistence of movement continuation is a characteristic that aids in the rhythmical establishment of a movement in the sense of repetition and periodicity. Rhythmic movement easily becomes habitual and automatic, and that is important in the development of a perfected technique. It is only when skills become automatic that they can be relegated to the lower centers, leaving the higher centers free for the creative and artistic factors of expression.

One of the most vital factors in dance is the physical, sensuous effect of rhythmic motion. When made too insistent, however, it is likely to pile up more emotional energy than can be satisfied —and be carried to the point of explosion.

One of the most perplexing problems in obtaining sincerity of feeling and clarity of communication is that of conveying the emotion that is central to the dance. Inexperienced dancers often give evidence of intellectual comprehension and may have a real appreciation of the technical problems involved and of the emotional significance of the content that is to be danced; yet this comprehension has little effect on their ability clearly to objectify in movement what has laid hold of their understanding. This difficulty frequently lies in the inability to perceive the adequate rhythmic forms as a correlate of the emotion being expressed. Rhythm is the primary, fundamental art form; its study is essential to all art, but especially to dance because of the latter's kinesthetic basis of perception. Because its regulating, stimulating powers are present in all that we think, feel, and do, it is imperative that we have some concept of it as a force.

Rhythm is difficult to define. Its significance is arrived at only by actually experiencing it. Whenever we experience rhythm in action, we usually describe it by saying the movement "felt right" or "had a swing." Rhythmic sensations feel right because of the right proportioning of the time and stress values that bind all the related parts into a unified experience sensed as a whole. This regulating and binding force is rhythm.

Organically, rhythm is a fundamental tendency in all our responses and is a principle of action in our physical organism. It is an attribute of man's nature. It is a constant principle of muscular action, which is control and release, work and rest, and is the only form in which muscular action can take place. Rhythm manifests itself in muscular tensions, and the mind becomes aware of this force by means of the kinesthetic sense. Movement implies energy release, and, because movement takes place according to laws of structural functioning which have a natural timing setup, rhythm as an experience may be said to be measured energy.

The organic characteristics of rhythm are also present in other forms of natural activity, such as thinking and feeling, which also proceed by rhythmic pulsations. The rhythms of song and poetry and the cadences of speech are as much manifestations of organic rhythm as breathing, walking, or any other muscular action.

Expressive movement is obviously rhythmical, not only because of structural patterning, but because of the influence on its form by thought and feeling, both of which fall into responsive rhythms.

In relation to organization, rhythm may be considered as the process by which events taking place in time are marked off, related, and organized. Without it all would be confusion. But the fundamental object of rhythm is to minister both to the stimulation and to the expression of feeling. Thus rhythmic form is the channel for reflecting mental experience. To a certain extent the rhythm of emotion determines the rhythm of motion.

So it is very unlikely that the internal rhythms of any two individuals are the same. In fact, the individual variations of the basic rhythmic patterns are what give unique value and interest to every student's expression. If inner and outer rhythm are one, communication is rich and complete; if not, the dance is likely to be too physical, too much of the body, rather than of the mind through the body. The source of this union between feeling and movement is a sensitive comprehension of idea, mood, rhythm, and movement.

Rhythm is also a potent source of inspiration. From the rhythms of his own bodily action, or from the rhythms of music and poetry, and from rhythms of activity in his environment, a dancer may derive his themes.

Any one of our senses may be employed in the perception of a rhythmic experience. Just as we are able to recognize a rhythmical sequence through the auditory sense, so we can learn through the kinesthetic sense to be aware of muscular sensations in terms of their duration and degrees of stress or force. It is this sense that informs us of the positions of the body and its parts, of the amount of effort and speed necessary for execution. Consciousness of meaning in movement comes through knowledge of its range, varying degrees of force, time relationships, and speed. In experiencing these rhythmic phases we produce a fundamental and ele-

DANCE: A CREATIVE ART EXPERIENCE

mental response, primarily organic, secondarily intellectual and discriminating. It is through the medium of these fundamental responses and their resulting stimuli of association that these structural factors arouse imaginative and emotional responses. In such a process there is involved a subtle creative manifestation of the feeling life. Thus we see that by rhythm much more is implied than just keeping time. In its broadest meaning rhythm may be said to be the mold through which expressive life flows in creating its forms. In dance, movements are the motor symbols of actions within the mental life of the dancer. Through action, dance expresses feeling aroused by the sensations of movement.

The dynamic phases of rhythmic movement may in brief be said to be: *duration,* or the relative length of time taken by any single movement; *stress,* or the degree of force or intensity with which energy is released; and *tempo,* or the rate at which movements follow one another. A series of movements may be executed in slow or rapid tempo without affecting the relative time of the single constituents, but change in tempo will bring about a change in the kinesthetic experience. These three phases of movement, all of which exist together in any action series, and out of whose interrelations the endless variety of dance patterns are built, determine the outward form of the dance; and in them are inherent the dynamic, generating causes of expression. Just as every animal has an action and a rhythm peculiar to itself, so man moves according to his nature. Every emotion has its appropriate and peculiar movement. There is movement of joy, rage, excitement, sorrow, peace, fear, devotion, and so on through the list of feeling

88

states. Movement, as outward, observable behavior, is an integration of the emotional, intellectual, and physical natures. Action implies a desire (emotion) which prompted it, a thought (intellect) which shaped it, and a visible movement of physical body to carry it out. That is to say, a desire stimulates a thought, and the thought embodies itself in an act. Two of these component activities are invisible and belong to the consciousness, but they are revealed by the third component, which is visible and belongs to the body. Mental states can be expressed only by actions, and can be communicated through their visible, characteristic attributes in the observable body. The development and control of the skill necessary for this body expression come through kinesthetic perception. To gain this power of discrimination, one must give attention to muscular sensations, and this study must be reinforced by understanding of the basic principles of motion. As an aid to efficiency, therefore, although not as a complete method, some sort of systematic body training is necessary. It is difficult in practice to separate the elements of physical skill in dance from its ideal essence, although it is clear in theory that movement is not art until it is emotionally charged and controlled by intellectual discipline.

It is clear, too, that the perfection of the body must mean more than the development of muscles and nerves; it must mean also a trained, enriched attitude of the whole human being. At the same time the value of gymnastic exercises should be recognized. From exercise and directed study the student can deduce rules which will be highly corrective while they are also formative. He will discover in his own experience ways and means which will take a significant part in producing satisfying art and which could not be taught from the outside. Out of such studies a rich and varied vocabulary of responsive movements comes automatically into play, and the form of movement, grounded in artistic intellectual selectivity, will be reflective of the emotions which cause it.

Technical Achievement

To develop a motor technique, and a fine discriminating kinesthetic sense to control it, is one of the solutions to the problem of dance education. It is a process of discovery, analysis, and synthesis, and a perfecting, according to an intellectual ordering, which demands the best efforts of both mind and body. The mental effort required to obviate mistakes demands so much concentration that other factors, such as expression, are bound to suffer. Repeated activity becomes automatic and is finally executed with little or no thought, thus freeing the mind for the activities of artistic creation. The impulses still pass over the original paths involving the cortex, and, although the latter does not attend fully, any error is quickly detected. Sensing something wrong, the mind becomes aware of it and makes corrections. These pathways of transmission do not come into existence as new and distinct entities. They arise from a general field of organic activity by a process of specialization; the result is a "specialized emergence." The onset of a stimulus results in a general bombardment of the nervous system, and out of this generalized activity there emerge the specialized paths we term skills. In this respect, all motor techniques are the same. Physical skill has the same general conditions whether it is concerned with tennis, swimming, dance, the playing of an instrument, or the handling of tools. Technique of the physical instrument is motor intelligence. Its acquirement is dependent upon intelligence and purpose and not upon mechanical drill or application of formula. Dance technique is the dancer's artistic integrity working through his nerves and muscles.

But to acquire technique one must first have desire, must "want to." The very inception of achieving is wanting to achieve. Indifference and accomplishment can never exist side by side. The greater the interest, the keener is our power. We are possessed to find out the hows and whys. Intellectual curiosity does not permit any rest until there is a solution. An indifferent attitude, or one of mechanically plodding along the line of least resistance on the chance that something may happen, will not bring perfection. The success of any act, no matter how simple or complex, depends upon a conscious direction of effort toward the ideal. Exactness in details, as opposed to slackness in the early stages, is essential. A desired result can be produced only by the perfecting of its elements. In the learning of any new act or movement, every sensation must be observed and registered, so that action becomes associated with certain effects in consciousness. These impressions, at the next effort of reproduction, will be useful in duplication of the effort or in avoidance of duplication according to one's abilities in recognition, comparison, analysis, and synthesis. When acts are performed consciously, the differences in action and effect can easily be noted. Such a worker will remember what was done, for he was conscious not only of what he was doing but of why!

Although the will is of importance in the expressive act, it can never be a substitute for the impulse to expression. The will is ever present, but blended with intellectual, emotional, and spiritual actions in a perfect unity. This blend of mental forces results in a kind of superintelligence that knows the effect before it starts the cause. This co-operation with the other mental faculties is one of the secrets of success. The will can control and guide, but never can supply the impulse to expression except as it serves mental concentration. In this capacity it holds the mind to the idea in hand, directing and restraining impulses until they become diffused through the whole organism. It collects a scatterbrain and makes an artist of the artisan. When the mind is so possessed, the force of its imagery tends to release itself over some motor path and becomes objectified in movements of dance. Here the will ceases to function and joins forces with the activity of the other mental actions concerned in expression. The true impulse to expression is deeper than the will. Unless the spirit commands the will and furnishes the motive to will or to express, expressive results are in danger of being superficial and limited. Power of expression depends upon power of thought and feeling. Nothing is detected so quickly as the resolution to be expressive and to appear emotional. Technique and expression really become one and the same thing, if we think of technique as the only adequate means of expression. Developing technique means directing and changing the untrained, seemingly natural, movement patterns into their related art forms.

The word *natural,* however, is an unfortunate word that has crept into dance parlance. It has come to be almost synonymous with that which is formless and without discipline. The natural should mean the perfect state. In this light, *correct* might be substituted for *natural.* So few people have developed, without training, the control necessary for good body motion; consequently the first step is to train back to the natural or correct way of moving. This is the only basis upon which consciousness of art movement can be established. But we must remember that patterns of the individual are revealed in the faulty, habitual movement. Every movement reveals organic unity because of its origin. In working toward a perfected technique we consciously direct untrained, unstudied movement into forms that aim toward a goal. The original, more instinctive form becomes conditioned by the ideal form. And only as the mind can conceive of these new forms as related to the familiar organic forms will a true and expressive style develop. The vitality of a movement is closely bound to the instinctive form which has arisen from the "life unity." Therefore, it is subject to, and controlled by, deep-seated influences that are of, and for, the organism. In building technique, then, we should try not to thwart and block the familiar reaction tendencies, but to release them in order that they may contribute to, and co-operate with, the goal-aiming efforts of the mind. If the aim is not uppermost, spontaneity will be lost because of distrust in "instinctive inspiration." Organic unity between inner and outer experience must not be destroyed. New forms should mean growth within the life pattern, not the destruction of it. This kind of effort, or technique, when workin   he ordinary toward the ideal, causes the body to take on an a.. ct impersonal quality resulting in an innate, unsought classical beauty.

Knowledge and Expression

Everyone brings to such a study some general but inarticulate understanding with which to build. But with a recognition and application of clear and exact principles, he can approach a scientific study of movement. There must be an understanding of the fundamental science of movement before the skill for its control can develop. No artist can afford to let temperament come between him and the facts which condition his work. The essence of science is the discovery of the truth of actual conditions. This discovery provides the knowledge and security with which any artist or student artist may work. There need be no antagonism between science and art. Science will not make art—but it will contribute to a truthful art. It is of the greatest importance, when we are working toward art expression, to know the conditions under which the mind creates and the nature of the medium through which it works. Our reactions are so likely to be fleeting and uncaught. We must, to be true to experience, be reinforced with understanding. Through analysis of conditions that contribute to expression comes the necessary understanding by which we gain clearer consciousness of our abilities as well as a keen appreciation of the efforts of others. But too much analysis may obscure the real significance of reality—something may escape, so that in the reconstruction there is less of substance than in the beginning. Also, we may become so engrossed in facts that we lose the vision of the finished whole, and thus the emergence of ideas that give significant meaning and value to facts is blocked. But, if analysis is used with the right understanding and emphasis, something more should result—an enrichment by understanding and confidence. We analyze to solve a problem, to find a solution or interpretation. We start with a complex, whole situation which must be explained. The elements are merely the result of analysis, discovered and abstracted for a greater appreciation of their relation to the whole. It is useful and helpful to separate the elements and to contrast one influence with another—for elements are simpler and more easily understood when taken as individual units. There is no danger in this process if we continually realize that the real phenomenon resides in the whole—which is something more than the sum of its parts. Analysis proves its usefulness when separate elements fuse into one impression. The earlier observations are not lost, though they no longer stand out as separate judgments; rather they have gone to enhance the total impression. Analysis then ceases to function; it is as if everything had been clear from the beginning.

In art, all knowledge must ultimately become intuitive. Every form of information should be so absorbed and transformed by the personality that the artistic expression which has grown out of that knowledge seems to be the inevitable product of spontaneous impulses. Such is the effect of the very greatest works, the works of supreme art.

For dance to be vital to an individual life its technique must be experienced in a way that recognizes the anatomical, physiological, and psychological connections and disciplines. It should be conceived in terms of those experiences that lie within the realm of the intellect, emotions, and spirit, and not in terms of arbitrary skills and forms except as they assist the function of expression and communication.

In the end, everything depends upon the individual. The instructor can give reasons *for*, can show *how*; but, when it comes to the act itself, the results will depend upon the student's advancement in control and artistic integrity and his potentialities as an artist. It is best, as well as inevitable, that such should be the case; for, when the body moves according to its structural principles, it moves like all other bodies and suggests the same forms. But, when movement is submitted to the dictates of an individual intellect and emotion, it ceases to be mechanically determined and becomes a manifestation of a unique and individual being.

Everyone inherits, basically, the same fundamental and primary nature. Through a fundamental and universal education this primary nature will be understood as the plane where instinctive impulses operate, and where impulses will be understood as powerful motives to action. And, finally, these forces will be trained to serve the will and desires of an intellect impelled by ideas so that the individual student can bring all his powers to bear upon the life of his choosing.

Of course, we can dance and teach dancing without knowledge concerning the setup that governs our responses. Very effective techniques of movement can be learned by prescription and imitation, and, because of the innate pleasure in obeying the impulse to move, such learned movements may well be pleasurable and satisfying. But, if imitation and prescription are too much relied upon, they are likely to cause the student to lose initiative and to become too mechanical, disarranging his individual adjustment rather than correcting it. Imitative activity very seldom gets the same results as inner creative activity. However, if imitation is used so as to start the inner activity of changes, it can be helpful and stimulating to new experiences—otherwise the essences of what is being imitated are missed. Conscious imitation as blind copying, however, is usually stilted and artificial. A student should be taught to teach himself. It is only as he is able, through his own effort to apply, to assimilate, and to ponder what he has learned that he is truly benefited. To attain genuine and convincing expression the creative mind needs to be permitted to organize and endow its materials with a specific structure and individuality.

To appreciate the origin and nature of dance, to understand the workings of its psychophysical-anatomical instrument, and to be convinced of its potentialities for emotional enrichment and self-direction, is to know the fundamental truth and enduring values of dance.

Chapter 5

FORM AS ORGANIC UNITY

*Form in any art rests upon a
deeply rooted principle that is
based upon the same biological
foundation as human behavior
and activity.*

THE FOLLOWING chapters on form will be more readily understood if we state at the outset how the term is here used.

If we grant that everything (whether a material object, such as an apple, or an idea, mood, or image of the mind) has form, a shape or defining characteristic by which it is known, then form is the "appearance" in which an external or internal experience presents itself.

In order to have external, observable form, an art must use some medium, which, in dance, is movement. To exist as an art form, this motor activity must be associated with imaginative content and mental discipline. This necessity presents two phases belonging to art form. One is the unseen, inner dance, which is the organization of the mental attributes into content; the other is the outer, observed dance, which is the result of the organization and execution of the motor elements. When the fusion of inner and outer experience is attained, form is achieved in its fullest meaning as *art form*.

In the last analysis we can say that form in all its implications means organization.

The particular way in which all the contributing elements, physical and psychical, are selected, organized, and manipulated, constitutes *style*.

Now let us first consider form generally, as *organic unity*.

If dance is to express emotional experience by means of visible motor symbols, obviously its movement forms must have reference to the forms of the related activities in experience. So form is a characteristic of all that we experience as well as a characteristic of that which expresses experience, and the two are organically related.

We are too inclined, perhaps, to think of form as belonging only to that part of a dance which can be seen—that is, its movements—and to neglect to go deeper and discover that form in any art rests upon a deeply rooted principle that is based upon the same biological foundation as are all forms of human behavior and activity.

Wherever there is life, there is an organic tendency to form. It is a creative tendency determined by the laws and forces of life itself. The forms of plants and the movements of animals and human beings as well as their biological functioning are the results of an inner determining activity. But man goes further. He of all creatures is destined by the very laws of his nature to achievements of another order. Unlike the animal, he is driven by convictions and ideas of the perfect that are not innate, but are the results of experience and education. How much simpler life would be if the development of an individual to his fullest psychophysical stature were as simple as that of the plant and animal, whose development is determined by an instinctive ordering. But the expressive forms of man's ideals and visions nevertheless are organically related to an inner activity. It is a property of the human organism to take the raw materials of sensation as unorganized energy, and to organize and relate them, thus endowing experience with a structure and individuality of its own.

In such a process, life patterns are constructed, and observable behavior becomes the form of their expression. If the concept of organic form is applied to all that man thinks and executes, we can see how significant its application is to his works of art. Any work of art, to be significant and convincing, should grow from what its creator has within, growing and changing as the germ idea changes. Visual appearance is then the result of inner impulsions and is genuine in conception. As has been said, man can fashion only as he knows. Art is but a fashioning from life, and life is a progressive scale of values, developed from experience, which becomes more and more enlightened by experience and the developing intellect.

The notion of visible form as organic unity, when applied to art activity, helps us to understand why, at the different so-called stages of cultural development, we have such varying art forms. The growing artist, like the developing race, passes through progressive levels of artistic achievement. Such a progression may be traced in the evolution of the dance. For convenience of discussion a series of three steps is suggested by which we may trace the growth of dance from its rudimentary forms to its more mature adult forms.

The first stage is elemental and highly sensory. The pleasure is in movement for the pure joy received from the sensation of moving. The movements typical of this stage are large, free, and untrained. Their execution demands little or no formal preparation. They display an instinctive skill that comes without instruction. Their shape is determined by the unrestrained rhythmical functioning of the body instrument rather than by an effort of the mind toward a form ideally conceived. Action here is the product of a mind unaware as yet of the intricacies of its medium. It is waiting on experience. It is becoming observant. It has still to gather experience, which in turn will be transformed into knowledge for later uses. There is no formal technique because the need for formal technique has yet to be sensed. Neither is there a serious attempt at unity and organization for permanency. This is dance in its infancy.

The dances evolved in this first stage are vital and exuberant. Their movements serve more as a release for physical and emotional energy than as a conscious expression of feeling. They have quality of a kind. We delight in them because of their spontaneity and vigorous rhythmic activity.

Little by little the evolving self outgrows this stage. It begins to gain a sense of security in the elemental phases of movement. The mind's need for order begins to assert itself and must be gratified. And so we enter the second stage.

There is now an attempt at unity and organization for permanency. The mind modifies its first abandonment. It becomes aware of the cause and effect of movement. Feeling and experience deepen. Along with experience comes an enrichment of reactions, accompanied by associated reasoning and thinking. In colloquial phraseology, we begin "to get wise to ourselves." Mind is being more and more employed to think about things that just happen, thus modifying behavior and developing a sense of values. Motor responses used in the first stage are likely to become upset, not only by new and heretofore untried motor controls, but by new emotional urges demanding expression as a result of new feeling states.

New controls are needed for the discipline and guidance of this enriching motor and sensory experience. The results are an increased interest in technique and a spirit of inventiveness. Movement becomes more disciplined, more subjective, and therefore more expressive. Not only is keen interest displayed in control of movement, but there is also an interest in seeking organization for its own sake, as well as in the pleasure derived from sensing unity. Dance is growing up.

As we pass from the second to the third stage in dance, mind becomes intellect. This stage is characterized by the development of the technique necessary to the expression of a maturing mind.

In the more adult dance a refined system of experiencing gradually evolves. Spontaneity is recovered, with the additional advantage of right principles of action instead of the undisciplined abandonment so typical of the earlier stages. There is rather a spiritual release of inhibiting forces. The survival values of the earlier experiences are not lost but are incorporated in the new. They undergo a process of refining as the mature aesthetic nature seeks to communicate itself. At the same time the unfolding mind has become a storehouse of experience. It has developed the capacity to select and formulate meanings. It has passed from sensing, to thinking, to knowing, and to willing.

And now dance has come of age. In this stage the dancer

organizes movement in order to give his meaning form. Through the expression of the emotional consciousness a complete psychic integration takes place.

It should be realized that, although dance reaches its highest art form in this stage, each stage produces dances that are characteristic of it and organically related to it. We must not lose sight of this fact, or we may make the mistake of comparing the products of one stage with those of another. The dances that emerge from each of these levels can be appreciated only as they are understood in terms of the conditions producing them. At all stages the process is creative—each stage evolving its own form at its own level. Too often inexperienced dancers are forced to express experiences and use forms of a more advanced level. To be fruitful, artistic growth must begin with fundamentals. In order to lay the background for the next stage, so that one stage may develop normally into the next, we must provide the proper nourishment at every level of growth. Unless such a progression is provided, either discouragement or superficiality will result.

We must not suppose, because artistic growth has been presented as developing on different levels, that progress goes on in this stratified fashion. Indeed, to some degree, all phases are occurring at the same time as the organism acts as a whole. The three stages might be considered as three accentuations and accumulations of the growing and developing aesthetic nature. The problem of creative teaching is to build the necessary background for progression and to provide ample opportunity for spontaneous emotional response. The development of skill and the appreciation of form must keep pace with the growing and inquiring intellect. Progress in dance requires ceaseless effort if we are to build a solid emotional, intellectual, and technical foundation upon which to erect a superstructure of artistic achievement. Those destined to be our artist dancers have an endless task in creating the particular style by which they may be best understood and enjoyed.

For convenience let us assume that the dancer's growth evolves from dancing for the sheer joy of sensing movement, to the seeking of form and mastering of technique, and to dance as the expression and communication of sensory experience, emotion, and creative imagination. But all must be subjected to an intellectual ordering. The mind likes organization and delights in obeying the impulse to gratify it. A tendency toward form is innate. Through the centuries man has accumulated a mass of "form experience" and has developed a keen sensitivity to order. From this innate urge toward form has emerged an aesthetic appreciation of it.

Art is ever the same, the effort of mankind to represent and interpret life. Only its forms change. As an age or an individual accumulates more experience, new meanings dawn upon the mind, releasing new intellectual forces, and from these are liberated the accompanying emotions. New forms must then be discovered to express adequately the newly sensed emotions. So it goes, in a constant transformation revealing change due to growth.

Organic form is significant form. It is a fusion of outward form with inner imagery.

Chapter 6
FORM AND CONTENT

> The inner, unseen dance is an embodiment of emotional experience unified by the organization of contributing psychological elements.

THE DISCUSSION of form so far has been rather general. The attempt has been to establish a broad concept of its meaning and to point out the distinction between the inner and the outer dance, as well as to establish the organic relation between the two. Each phase has its particular materials that must be organized.

A dance begins with impressions, with sensory or psychic images which may be subjective or objective in origin. We may dance our feelings about ourselves, about our fellowmen, or about the nature of the universe as we feel and know it. Whatever the source of the impressions, from the moment of their reception they become subjective and personal. They take new character from the receiving personality. Thus all imagery is an individual transformation of original stimulation. If the image of a dance were an exact and unfiltered return of experience, it would indicate a very neutral relation of the personality to life. Such a mind, in dealing with experience, would show but little resistance or selection.

But what is the nature of an experience that impels its expression, and what are the conditions of entering into the creative art activity by giving an experience an expressive form?

Aesthetic Experience

The kind of experience capable of producing a dance, or any work of art, is one that causes us to react in a special way. This special way is the *aesthetic way*.

Unfortunately, aesthetic experience is too often considered as divorced from the capacities of the ordinary person. To enjoy, to desire, and to feel pleasure and satisfaction are very human capacities. Broadly speaking, the many experiences that bombard us during the day could be judged aesthetically if we were capable of taking a detached attitude toward them and of evaluating them as experience, judging them according to their own standards. What usually happens to prevent such a response is that we are more concerned with the total effects of the particular event upon us. We permit other judgments and considerations to prevent the aesthetic judgment from existing as a single experience. For example, we may be witnessing a destructive fire. If we consider the grief and loss it is causing, we are likely not to enjoy the fire as a gorgeous blaze. The enjoyment of the blaze as a thrilling spectacle would be the aesthetic experience, no matter how great the catastrophe. And, too, the evaluation would depend upon what we consider a good blaze, which in turn is dependent upon how many fires we have experienced to form the basis of comparison. In so far as the demands for what we consider a good fire are met, we say it is a beautiful fire.

Things, circumstances, character, ideas, objects of art—all seem beautiful to us when they have a value for us. Satisfaction and beauty are qualities not of objects and events, but of an individual way of experiencing them. In observing a dance or a painting or any work of art, we may not be aware of the specific purpose intended by its creator—but it is present and actively exerting its influence. We find beauty only in terms of our ability to discover it; that is, we project into the particular dance those feelings of beauty which have been aroused and at the same time satisfied within us. To enter into an aesthetic experience through dance is to find satisfaction for the aesthetic sense of what we think beautiful movement should be. Under these circumstances we say "it is beautiful." What really has happened is that the dance has met the needs and demands of our aesthetic judgment.

An absolutely pure aesthetic experience is perhaps possible only to the child and to primitive natures which are free to enjoy the sensations of mere perception untrammeled by any other consideration than the experience for its own sake. As we mature, different values emerge in our developing nature, varying from those satisfactions met by our physical needs to those needs of the higher social, mental, and spiritual natures.

With the amassing of experience, the maturing mind becomes aware not only of relations existing between objects, events, and ideas but of their values. Reason enters into this emerging relational consciousness and causes other judgments to appear. The result is that the aesthetic judgment is lifted from the level of instinct and elemental feeling to that of intelligence and understanding.

It is in this way that thinking affects our behavior (artistic and otherwise), for it directs action toward the goal of a consciously determined purpose. The fullest appreciation, however, goes beyond mere pleasurable reactions. It also includes the capacity for idealization—that ability of the creative and inventive imagination to construct something new out of the materials of sensation. It is when the mind makes sense out of the sensation of movement that movement becomes transformed into expressive art movement.

Although aesthetic experience contains important intellectual elements essential to appreciation, it remains nevertheless primarily a feeling experience. It seems that there is something in the original nature of man that leads to immediate pleasure in some responses without the intervention of the more rational processes, and it is upon this basic tendency to pleasurable responses that art education should be built. Mere sensation is not sufficient—emotional consciousness is needed; and observation requires appreciation. These factors determine the conditions and meaning of value.

Value does not exist apart from some appreciation, and no good exists without some preference. An object is good to us because it is of value to us, because we desire it, rather than that we value it because it is good. Preference must include those judgments that are instinctive and immediate, pleasurable and painful. Pleasure, however, that comes from selection and contemplation, though based on these unlearned capacities of our original nature, leads to a higher order of appreciation. Meanings and relations are grasped by the rational consciousness; but the values which art expresses are emotional values and are grasped by the emotional consciousness. Intellectual satisfaction may lead to aesthetic experience as well as emotional satisfaction. But a blending of the two will lead to a richer and more satisfying aesthetic experience. The complete and satisfying aesthetic experience needs both.

Not all aesthetic experience may be developed into an art experience, but no art experience can exist without aesthetic experience, which is the essential preliminary of the more deliberate and directed experience that becomes the substance of a work of art. Any experience, pleasant or unpleasant, can be an aesthetic experience, and as such its value resides in the value of its expression. That is, it is transformed into an object of beauty by the creative art activity.

Although the sensing of beauty is subjective and relative, the universal aspect of beauty and of the artistic appeal must not be overlooked. All experience, of course, is individual, yet we are sharers in common satisfactions, joys, sorrows, and pleasures. No matter how individual our feelings are, the thrill to the perfect is an experience common to many. We are social creatures and as such seek not only one another's company—but one another's approval. It is only the extreme individualist who can achieve complete independence of the influence of his fellowmen. Social inheritance and training have gradually evolved socialized artistic values (those values that have been recognized and accepted as giving the greatest satisfaction to the greatest number of those who are sensitive to, and appreciative of, artistic values). During the ages this has to a certain degree ensured an agreement as to that which is pleasing, satisfying, and admirable.

At the same time it must be remembered that during the ages ideas have changed. These changes are observed in form rather than in innate qualities. The history of taste, in civilizations as in individuals, is one of evolution. There is no growth

DANCE: A CREATIVE ART EXPERIENCE

apart from a purpose. In all works of art there is a motive underlying the act that produces them. No beautiful thing is created passively, indifferent to a purpose. If we can keep in mind the interplay between the social order and its individual elements, and realize that one is necessary to and cannot exist without the other, then we can understand how art education may be socializing, instead of thwarting and limiting, for it should free the individual to enjoy all that has been found good in the past as well as to enjoy the art creations of his own age.

The very source of aesthetic pleasure in movement is found in our physiological and psychological make-up. Activity itself is a physiological condition of pleasure. The mere sensation of moving is pleasurable to the organism. Not only does movement enhance pleasurable feelings, but pleasurable feelings tend toward increased activity. Also, movement relieves suffering. We know from experience and observation that, generally speaking, pain increases as inhibition increases and can be lessened by active manifestation. As Hirn says, it is "the life-preserving tendency which, under the feeling of pleasure, leads us to movements which intensify the sensation and make it more distinct for consciousness, compels us in pain to seek for relief and deliverance in violent motor discharge." * Under such conditions movements is expressional, but not yet a dance.

Every emotion, in contrast to the feeling states of pure sensation, is a highly complex state of consciousness involving intel-

* Yrjö Hirn, *The Origins of Art* (New York, 1900), page 42, by permission of The Macmillan Company, publishers.

lectual elements, a tone of pure feeling either pleasant or un-pleasant, and an inrush of somatic sensations due to the diffused nervous excitement. It is difficult to imagine any emotion that is not connected with feelings of bodily and motor sensations. Every feeling state has its motor phase, which is attendant upon physical as well as mental feeling.

During an individual life there is laid down a firm founda-tion for association between activity and its accompanying feel-ing states. So association must be considered as exercising an in-fluence on feelings and affecting the activities connected with them. The feelings that accompany activity are mental states that become recorded in the sentient being for future reference. They have been connected with situations or events that have stimulated activity. Therefore, the associations in turn take on the quality of the feeling tone aroused by the original stimulus. These feelings, which have become definitely associated with arousing situations, call for action or outward expression. But this is not yet a dance expression.

Although a dance is a consciously directed activity, it arises out of experiences of actual life that just happen to us and to which we respond in the passing according to our nature. It is the quality of this everyday experiencing that conditions the quality of aesthetic experiencing. It is its basis. So, in presenting dance as art experience, we must associate feeling and movement and at the same time select the significant phase of the motor response for artistic expression. By understanding the general feeling states that instinctively accompany action, we can bring about an emotional experience by recalling and experiencing its motor phase.

Like all works of art, a dance expresses emotions aroused by *images,* which are sensory or psychic, objective or subjective, in origin. Ideas and emotions, as we have seen, do not appear in the mind without some sensorial accompaniment. Sensation must first make its entrance before there can be perception and its accompanying feeling state. This is the image aspect of consciousness, whereas the resulting idea and its accompanying emotion are the meaning and significance of the image. People differ in their power and kind of imagery. Those who have strong auditory imagery retain more easily the sound aspect of experiences; those of the visual type attend more to what they see and think in terms of visual imagery; and those of the motor type respond more easily to the movement quality of experience. They think more in terms of images derived from movement. People who enjoy activity generally, and dancers in particular, are usually of the last type, and as dancers are endowed with vivid motor imagination and memory. (A dance remembered should mean a motor recall—the memory of tensions, and the feeling of the dynamic qualities of the acts involved.)

When the final image is clearly and vividly sensed, it demands release and tends to expel itself from the mind over the motor paths and find expression in movement. The strength of the emotional tone is dependent upon the clearness of the image, and the amount of image recall is dependent upon the wealth of the imaginal materials of the mind.

FORM AND CONTENT

The observable form is, therefore, biologic and organic, for it is an extension of inner conditions into their expressive form. The sources are life itself, and the life forces dictate the fashioning of the expressive medium.

There is a difference between emotion as it is experienced and released in our actual living and as it is experienced and expressed in dance. To writhe in pain or jump about for joy may be an expressive movement, but it is not a dance. In real life emotion is usually more intense than in artistic life, and it may be so intense as to dominate the person. Emotion derived from an image stimulus, on the other hand, can be more easily controlled and regulated. It is also usually clearer and better integrated with other energies of the mind, for, in art, experience and emotion are clarified by selection. To feel in dance as we do in direct experience would result in impulsive, unorganized, and too realistic movement. This should never be the case in art, in which emotion is not independent of thought and will, but co-operates with them. The attempt to express completely often causes an audience to become self-conscious and embarrassed because of an emotional nudity which can be made presentable only by abstraction and restraint. Artistic emotion is a controlled and selected image recall. A dance, of course, must be an individual thing, but not a personal thing; and a dancer must have the capacity of expressing human emotions without appearing to share them personally. A dance is an image stimulus.

From the mass of material that bombards him daily the dancer takes his inspiration. So, first of all, the mental experience consists of something which must initiate an aesthetic experience. Once an idea is seized upon, the creative process demands that it be prolonged in the imagination by concentrated attention, which causes it to become elaborated by all the associative processes of the mental life. It gathers round itself a great mass of associated imagery—stimulated by ideas, emotions, memories— all related to the original stimulating circumstance. The next step is to select, to abstract those elements that are most pertinent to the mental state seeking expression. And finally these essentials are combined and worked over into a newly constructed image. It is an imaginative elaborating of sense presentations; and, when the awakened emotions reveal within themselves meaning, order, and significance, they become substance ready to be expressed.

For a dance, then, to be composed there must first be something to dance about. And this something must be so valued that its worth is its value of expression. It may be occasioned by an event of outer or inner life. It may be discovered in the outside world of actual happening, or appear seemingly clearly formed from the deepest resources of the mind. It may be initiated by emotions aroused by the appreciation of universal harmony, by the immensity of space, or by the mystery of life and death. Such experiences usually inspire in us feelings of awe, dread, or reverence. Another group of impressions, such as vulgarity, injustice, and treachery, may excite feelings of contempt or disgust. And for comedy we have but to turn to the realm of human experience and observe man's behavior—his manners, foibles, and follies. Actions of animals also are a source of material that may be treated with varying degrees of humor—from comedy to satire to grotesquerie.

The accompanying feeling states may run the gamut from those we call pleasant to those we call painful. The pleasant, expansive mental states are those usually associated with joy, love, admiration, and hope—to mention only a few. They exhilarate and elevate the body. Unpleasant and contracting mental states are connected with fear, hate, envy, sorrow, despair, and humiliation. They are emotions that depress the body.

Manifestative and Representative Dances

There are many ways of reacting to whatever happens to us, and there are just as many ways of responding to it and expressing it. For our purposes we shall say that reaction to experience may be objective or subjective, depending on whether experience is directed away from or toward the self. That is, the objective way is more concerned with the object, or stimulating cause, while the subjective way is more concerned with the mental states which the cause arouses. The one is concerned more with things and facts, the other with meanings and feelings.

These different ways of experiencing suggest the terms *representative* and *manifestative* as the manner of their presentation. The *representative* way is a manner that appeals more directly to intellect and reason. It tends toward realism and description and stimulates the observer to conceive the object or thing as subject matter. Content as such becomes the issue rather than the subtle overtones that are caught in a more subjective way of experiencing. To express the latter values, the less literal manifestative way is used. *Manifestation* is more indirect and is concerned with "values sensed" rather than with "knowledge about." In proportion as the dance is representative, its meaning can be grasped at once. In proportion as it is manifestative, its meaning is realized more by the imagination. The two modes should be considered as essential elements of every good dance composition. Some representation must be present as a means of reference to the actual experience so that not all reality is lost. And the manifestative elements must be present so that what the aesthetic nature has valued will not be lost. However, only as much representation should be used as is necessary to aid the mind to grasp meaning. Obviously, the amount of representation and manifestation employed will be determined by the kind of subject matter chosen to be danced, by the purpose, and by the artistic integrity of the dancer. Both manners of treatment afford opportunity for artistic presentation.

Because of the presence of more obvious and realistic elements in the representative manner, dance is usually introduced to the less dance-conscious audience in this form. *Theater dance* is the term used for a dance manner designed for the entertainment of the theater audience. People go to the theater to partake of the emotional experience of the actors, musicians, and dancers. They want to understand and be moved as well as to be entertained. Dance moves too swiftly for its meaning to be grasped by the average audience. Until our audiences are more informed, it is essential that dance be presented as directly and vividly as possible.

To accomplish this, more realistic and pantomimic movement is used, as well as helpful properties. Although theater dance is not dance in its most highly developed art form, nevertheless it is a vehicle for great artistic treatment, and it will continue to be an important agent in educating audiences in dance appreciation.

Recital dance is the term that is used for the manifestative dance which approaches absolute dance—dance in its most highly developed form. Its movements depend less upon extraneous aid, such as pictorial, literary, or dramatic theme, to convey its message. Movement relies solely upon its own power to arouse emotive forces.

However, the chief requisite of dance as an art is expression and communication through movement, and it must not be too dependent upon expression through associated imagery. Its purpose is to execute movements whose dynamics and body positions embody expression and have the power to arouse similar forces in the onlooker. This means that we should be able to go to a dance recital for an aesthetic experience stimulated by movement, and not by music, stage setting, or costumes, except as they supplement and accompany movement. This, of course, is the ideal state, but not an impossible one. Whatever of meaning and value one finds in dance is largely a matter of education, experience, and personal idiosyncrasies.

Manifestative dances may be of two orders: dances of action, and dances of mood and emotions. By *dances of action* are meant those dances that have their source in feeling states of motor origin. Bodily activity awakens sensory processes leading to sensations that become the inspiration for a dance. Such a dance is not concerned with specific happenings, descriptions, life issues, or memories. Its movements are organized for no other reason than the rhythmic sense of free action and the satisfaction of their being given form. They are expressive of the beauty and rapture inherent in the movements used. Through action, a dance of this order is composed to express and communicate feelings of motor origin associated with the sensations of movements, and not as a motor expression of moods and emotions.

But sensations do not exist for their own sake. They have the function of representing things and of bringing images before the mind. Thus ideas of things become associated with sensations and endow them with meaning. These "ideas about" and "meanings of" in turn arouse definite feeling states, usually thought of as emotions. And although the mental states aroused by dances of action are naturally less complex than those having their inception in the feeling states associated with thought, they may, through association, appeal to the more intellectual and emotional aspects, and afford a very satisfying aesthetic experience.

An example of a dance of action is one that employs leaping and running for the sheer pleasure of leaping and the skill of defying gravity, and for the excitement of speed. Or again, movements that have a definite rhythmic scheme may be woven into a composition for the delight and enjoyment of the rhythm, such as a waltz, tango, mazurka, or polka. The action exists for action's sake, to delight the senses and charm the intellect, and not to leap, run, waltz, or polka with some ulterior purpose. The expressive quality of these dances depends upon the spontaneous animation of the dancer, for they are based on the rhythmic sensitivity and expressiveness of individuality. The dancer's spirit becomes animated and reacts to the stimulating effects of movement. Without this element, such dances would exist as a series of well-executed calisthenics and would have little value as art.

Dances of the second order of this classification, the dances of *mood* and *emotions*, resemble those of the first in that they, too, are subjective and without a story. They have their inception in a more complex mental state and, therefore, are arrived at in a slightly different manner. Instead of belonging to the sensory phase of experience they belong primarily to the emotional, but they have deep roots in the sensory and intellectual phases of experience.

Here the action of the muscles is under the influence of a strong emotional force. In the dances first mentioned, spontaneous expression seems to flow out of the present movement, whereas the movement of these dances exists as a symbol of the emotion. The movement sensations are under the modification of more complex mental processes. Consequently the muscle agitations are more complex and subtle. Both kinds of dances may have any flavor, from the comic to the tragic, suggesting a complete picture of gaiety, hope, despair, awe, or tranquillity. Manifestative dances partake of the lyric spirit, for here thought is penetrated more with feeling than with situation or event; and movement exists as the expression of an emotion or mood that is the dancer's own, and without reference to any cause.

DANCE: A CREATIVE ART EXPERIENCE

Abstract dances of great complexity are not possible to everyone. Highly developed emotions and sentiments are feeling states that exist only in the more mature minds; therefore their expression requires a more mature mental development and technical power of execution than do the more instinctive and less complex feelings. When working on dance content for composition, one should keep these factors in mind, so as to stay within the intellectual and emotional reach of the student. Emotive experience may be led up to and prepared, but feeling itself is stimulated only by vivid mental realization.

Representative dances may likewise be classified into two orders: thematic dances, and dances of characterization. *Thematic dances* are concerned with content that refers to some definite situation or story. It should be remembered that there are minds that find it difficult to grasp emotional content without seeing the definite cause that called the feeling into being. Generally speaking, most of our feelings, except the simplest organic ones, are induced by ideas of things. Consequently it often proves helpful to evolve a situation or sequence of events as a theme. The theme may be simple enough for a dance of a single interest, or sufficiently complex to take on the proportions of a dance drama. In either case, the dance movements depend upon a text containing some realistic human interest that kindles the imagination and arouses the emotions. Although these dances do not depict the situation literally, they do use sufficiently descriptive movement to suggest the situation, and thus approach the imaginal and emotional experiencing. Since the emotions are to be reached through ideas, the movements will be somewhat restricted by the necessity of following well-determined and definite reaction patterns. As has already been pointed out, these dances are objective and realistic and appeal more immediately to reason than to feeling and imagination.

The artistic success of the thematic dance depends upon the abstraction from the realistic situation of those elements that lend themselves to dance treatment. Otherwise the movements will be too literal and no longer exist as dance movement. Such dances are to the field of dance what program music is to the field of music. If representation is carried to the point where expressive movement is neither pure dance nor strictly pantomimic, but partakes of both, we may assign such dances to the marginal zone of *pantomimic dance.*

The second order of representative dances, *dances of characterization,* are those whose movements take on the qualities of another character. The creative imagination appropriates the experiences of another and enters into a point of view different from his own. The dancer "others" himself. He designs his movements to portray another's actions and feelings. Animals as well as people suggest a wealth of subject matter for characterization.

Representative dances partake of the dramatic spirit, for here thought is directed toward the particular situation that is depicted to evoke the desired emotional response, whereas manifestative dances express emotions directly without reference to a cause. They may, however, through association, suggest a story or situation and thus bring about a concrete interpretation.

Although we may not acknowledge the more representative

DANCE: A CREATIVE ART EXPERIENCE

dance to be as pure a dance manner as the more abstract manifestative dance, we must admit its important place in the evolving art life of the individual dance student and of the public as a
whole. It will take time to bring the public to a full appreciation
of absolute dance, and we must not be too intolerant and im-
patient.

This classification of dances has been suggested to avoid the
confusion resulting from the attempt to label dances as interpretative, dramatic, romantic, lyric, modern, aesthetic, and so
on. Such terms, however, do have suggestive significance, but in
their broadest meaning they could include all dances of artistic
value. On the other hand, if too narrowly defined, they are too
rigid and fail to be truly interpretative of any. If we keep in mind
that all dances of artistic intent are composed to express and communicate feeling states and ideas, we can avoid difficulty by dis-
tinguishing them in terms of the essential and characteristic mental experience they embody.

Before closing this chapter we shall attempt a definition of
dance that is sufficiently broad to include the many types of activity that lay claim to being dance. We may say, in the light of
what has gone before, that a dance is the rhythmic motor expression of feeling states, aesthetically valued, whose movement symbols are consciously designed for the pleasure and satisfaction of
re-experiencing, of expressing, of communicating, of executing,
·and of creating form. Such a statement includes the less mature
art forms, such as tap, group, and ballroom dancing, as well as the
more highly developed forms. All are stimulated by aesthetic ex-

perience of some kind which is expressed in movement. Movement itself is not the essence of motor expression. Dance demands that motor expression grow out of an emotional need. The need may be the desire to enjoy just the sensation of movement; or to re-experience the rhythmical pleasure of the waltz or any other ballroom step; or to tap out in well-organized and well-executed movements an intriguing rhythmical pattern; or to enhance one's pleasure in movement by participation in a group dance.

These forms, by their very nature, do not have as great a claim to being fine art as do those dances that are composed to express feeling states that have their inception in the higher mental and spiritual natures ("higher" only because of later development). Consequently, only dances expressive of these more complex emotional states have come to be regarded as having art value, whereas they are simply the expression of a more mature artistic nature. Unfortunately, *contemporary dance* has come to be synonymous with the more highly developed forms, though in all ages, and in accordance with all stages of development, dance exists in forms that are true art expressions of the conditions that produce them. And often *contemporary dance* and *modern dance* are terms that have come to mean only the personalized dance manner of contemporary artist dancers. But, if the more elementary and sensory dances are created and danced in a true creative art spirit, they too have their place in a larger concept of dance. When dance is understood in terms of its essential nature, its meaning will be broadened to include all forms that are created and executed in response to an impelling aesthetic need.

DANCE: A CREATIVE ART EXPERIENCE

As a dancer grows in sensitivity and freedom of spirit and develops more technique of execution, he will create dance themes from his own realm of experience, knowing what to select and how to choose its manner of presentation. He should be encouraged and directed toward utilizing the materials of his own experiences for aesthetic enjoyment and for imaginative reconstruction through the movements of dance. One of the chief aims of dance education should be the development of the individual's own aesthetic powers, with special emphasis on clear spontaneous feeling and on the ability to organize experience creatively. Students should be encouraged to become aware of nature and their social world, to look upon their own experiences with untrammeled vision, and through guidance and experimentation to discover the most appropriate mode of expression.

In building from the simple, immature beginnings to more finished art results, we must not lose sight of the importance of the elementary, sensorial type of human response. It is essentially physiological, and therefore primary, and it is natural to young children and unsophisticated adults. Because of the pleasant nature of the sensation, this type of response is spontaneous and demands little effort of attention. It is necessary, through the conditioning processes of education and training, to lead away from it and beyond it, but we must keep in mind that it is a physiological necessity and that it remains the indispensable source upon which later art developments depend.

Through the senses we receive impressions not only of our world, but of ourselves. With our intelligence we arrive at understanding and meaning; with the imagination we combine impressions; out of past experiences we create new images; and with our will and energy we execute and bring them into existence. This is the creative act.

Chapter 7
FORM AND STRUCTURE

Form as structure is the projection of forces within, into the outward form of their expression. It is the organization of motor elements into a meaningful, visible pattern.

THE IDEA of form becomes increasingly complex, for there must be not only unity of the psychological elements that give form to content, but also unity of the motor elements resulting in the observed structure. This observed form is what is usually thought of as *a dance;* and it is only by means of its outwardly constructed form that a dance is able to accomplish its dual purpose of expression and communication. It is through the visible form that the observer is brought into relation with the emotional and intellectual experience of the dancer. To compose is to produce what the mind has created.

The success of the structural phase depends upon the choice of movements, their organization, and their execution. First let us consider the choice of movement symbols used.

Although skillful and well co-ordinated movements are essential to dance, they will not assure its existence as an art form. For movement in dance is used as the medium of expression, and not as an activity executed for the exhibition of the functioning structure. Dance movements exist as acts that originate from spontaneous impulses, but they become modified by the informing mind as it molds and relates their forms to the end that there may be unity between movement and whatever of thought and feeling they are to embody. The dancer is given this very unity, for his tools are the expressive acts in which form and content have already been established, just as the poet is given unity in words and their meanings.

When we consider the firm foundation that is laid for association between feeling and activity during an individual life, we can appreciate how much influence association exerts on the feelings and on the activities connected with them. Movements have become meaningful not only through the process of association, but also through the rhythmical functioning of the body structure. Out of these untaught movement responses has evolved an appreciation of their characteristic forms and expressive mood values. Although the particular forms of movement response need not be identical, nevertheless there are constant fundamental elements of behavior that persist and cause movement to be understood.

These are the essentials of movement that are to be discovered, selected, and abstracted as the carriers of meaning, and that become organized into the final dance.

To illustrate: If a dancer wishes to dance her idea and feeling of a lullaby, it would not be the best art form if realistic movements of holding and rocking the child were used. But, if the positions of holding and rocking were suggested, and the essential rhythms of the lullaby behavior patterns were used for the rhythms of the dance movement, they would serve to suggest rather than produce the act itself.

By understanding the general feeling states that inherently accompany actions, we can bring about an emotional experience by recalling and experiencing its motor phase. Thus the physical form arouses the art experience. For a dance, the process of association is complete when its movements are quickened by, and reverberate with, the quality of the feeling state which causes its expression. It is when this quality enters into a movement experience that action which otherwise seems buried in technique becomes dancing. That is, movement becomes dancing when the mind makes sense out of motor sensation by endowing it with personal and artistic meaning. When a complete experience is intentionally given form in expressive movements, there results a dance.

So the particular problem of this phase of composing is the finding and working over of movements whose patterns and tensions, acting as emotive forces, will cause similar stresses and strains in the observer.

To this end the dancer employs distortion as a means to stimulate and heighten awareness of feeling states through the visual design of his movements. As a term, *distortion* is unfortunate, for it too often suggests the ugly and unnatural, instead of a necessary deviation from the normal. Dance, like all the arts, distorts, that is, exaggerates its medium for artistic effect and expressive purpose, that there may be a heightening of forces as a more effective stimulus. Distortion in dance might be thought of as hyperbole of movement—as an overstatement or understatement. If the movement forms executed were only those of ordinary movement experience, there would result not dance but a literal statement of events with no heightened feeling states. However, if movement is twisted and forced into patterns that are too unreal, and from which too much of the human element has been extracted, its communicative value is definitely weakened or lost. And, on the other hand, if movement is too realistic, it tells too much, leaving nothing to the imagination. But, when artistically used, distortion does not seem unnatural or incongruous, for it is rational to feeling. To employ distortion artistically, the dancer must first achieve an understanding and mastery of the normal. He is then free to deviate from it according to his artistic integrity.

Not only must a dancer be sensitive to effects achieved through exaggeration; he must also be sensitive to the linear qualities of the body in action. He must be *line-wise*.

We are accustomed to think of line as a quality of the more graphic art forms, rather than of so fleeting a medium as movement. Yet movement is capable of linear design, which, if properly employed, can greatly enhance its effectiveness. For sense of line gives to movement qualities which in themselves suggest an emotional meaning. Our response to this quality in actions may be due to an unconscious association with our sensations of the gravity axes. There are feelings of repose, serenity, strength, and breadth in the horizontal. The piercing, ascending path of the vertical imparts the feeling of power, dignity, and spiritual strength. The curved and sinuous lines impress with their charm and grace and effortless flow of movement. Because of our ability to sympathize muscularly, we read ourselves into the lines and observe how it would feel to move in their paths.

It is essential for the dancer to become line-wise, not only as a matter of direction when he is moving through space, but for the purpose of imparting a linear significance to the body and its parts while they are in action. He should be able to dispose the straight and curved lines of his moving body in such a way as to evoke sensations and associations that are peculiar to them. There is life in line, and, when used as an artistic tool, it can enhance the communicative power of movement. For high artistic achievement, a consciously directed linear treatment requires a very discriminating sense of line and of the dynamic values latent in linear form, as well as the ability to point up the essential phase of a movement phrase, by which is meant the checking or crystallizing of a movement at its climax, suggesting the completed action without abandoning it to its full range of action. If not skillfully handled, movement so treated is likely to result in a dance that is nothing more than a series of static positions. This is because the pictorial effect becomes an end in itself, instead of being the capturing of motion at the one point that is the culmination and expression of its evolutions. Line and pattern in movement are a necessary and vital aid to emotional transmission, but they should not be permitted to dominate other factors of composition.

Sensitivity to *space* is another important factor contributing to the emotive power of movement. Essentially it is an awareness of the variety of directions that the body and its parts can take when moving through space. It is a feeling of "out-thereness." It is a sense of relationship between the self and space, considered as extensiveness rather than as something having boundaries. For the dancer this latter consideration refers to the patterns existing in space, whose shapes are determined by the varying postures the body assumes while in action.

The idea of space forms may also refer to the floor patterns made by the feet as they propel the body through space, or to those paths made by any moving part of the body, such as the head, arms, trunk, or legs. These space factors have within them power to contribute much to the aesthetic effect of the final synthesis.

In molding the visual design of the individual movements by employing the various factors inherent in movement, such as line, speed, force, rhythm, and time-space, we must not forget that they are expressive in themselves of a vague way of feeling. They have their emotive concomitants, for they are the factors that arouse glandular and general body changes such as are revealed by quickened or retarded breath and pulse. Their reactions are primarily organic, but have power to stimulate the imaginative and emotional natures. Therefore they should be so used that the feeling tone of their forms will be identical with that of the content they are to embody. That is, the form of the movement patterns must be so constructed and executed that they will re-express the meaning of the content.

Once the desired movements have been discovered, they must be so organized that the newly formed whole answers to the mind's need for ready comprehension.

To accomplish *organization* or structure by aiding the comprehending mind to grasp meaning, the same devices are used as in everyday intercourse. If we spoke or wrote with our words all jumbled into incoherent groupings without thought of order and relative positions, there would be no communication. A dancer goes to work in much the same way as he fashions his speech and writing. He sets out to assemble, relate, and integrate his materials into the final expressive whole.

This structural process is consciously performed, and its desired end is *unity*. Unity, although an organization of many parts, is an entirety, a wholeness, so organized that nothing can be added or taken away without damage to the whole. This unity depends upon several operative forces. Within it there must be *variety* and *contrast*, so that the parts are thrown into relief by juxtaposition, thus adding to interest and enhancement. If variety is sought for variety's sake, irrelevant elements are likely to be introduced, and *balance* may be sacrificed because of the lack of proper proportion between the parts.

The movements must build to a *climax*. There must be a beginning, a rise to the turning point, and a resolution. As the plan develops, it is carried forward by sheer momentum of action. Stress in rhythm, strength in action, and varying shades of feeling are factors that contribute to the richness and animation of any dance composition.

Organization demands a *sequence* of the movements employed —an order in which one movement follows another. It is more than a mere arrangement. A single movement is potentially expressive in itself, but, unless placed in juxtaposition to other movements that form a larger expressive unit or phrase, it is not significantly expressive—just as a single note cannot, by itself, be a melody. It is this contiguity, this necessary closeness, of one movement to another that distinguishes sequence from arrangement.

The manner in which a movement grows out of, or follows, the preceding one, and the way in which phrases are tied together or related, is the problem of *transition*. Although transition is spoken of as a matter of execution, its need is included within structure.

Repetition is necessary to bring to a focus those parts that are dominant and that are meant to give special significance to the whole. It is perhaps the most primal principle in all rhythmic structures. We find it in the periodicity and recurrence of accent. In some of its uses its effect is hypnotic, and, when made too insistent, it is likely to generate more emotional energy than can be satisfied, and often an explosion results. However, only the too uniform rhythms that demand too little or no effort of the mind lead to difficulty. As long as effort is directed toward an ideal and a purpose, satisfaction rather than excitement will result.

Good composition demands that there be a *harmonious* working together of parts. Nothing must be out of key or in an unrelated key. This means that identical qualities and purpose should be embodied in the various elements.

And, finally, there should be no neglect of seemingly less important parts. Although some movements will seem to be of more importance than others, and receive more attention, those of less interest should not be slighted. Every part, no matter how small, is a means to the fulfillment of the desired end, and as such is important. Care for details is characteristic of all great works of art.

As intellectual and unemotional as these principles of composition may seem, they are structural constants that are the very heart of dance composition. Their great communicative necessity and expressive significance are clear to the dancer and the understanding critic. The principles of variety, contrast, balance, climax, sequence, transition, repetition, and harmony, all aiming at unity, can be modified but never abandoned.* The mind must express itself logically and can comprehend meaning only when elements are arranged in a telling and meaningful form. It is the proportion and manner in which the elements are combined according to these principles that constitute the character of the final form.

For example, music gives us certain standardized ways of handling its materials—such as the fugue, rondo, and canon forms—each having characteristics peculiar to its own form. They are formulae that have been tried and found good, and they afford excellent examples of the operative forces contributing to structural form.

Traditional and accepted forms and standards, even though superior to the student's work, should be presented for analysis and comprehension to aid the student in finding the solution of his own problems. Regimentation is fatal to progress and initiative. However, it is also fatal to leave students unguided and uninspired. The desire and interest of the inexperienced may not be sufficiently impelling to overcome inertia and difficulties and to launch them into new activities. The danger here is that restrictive habits may be formed, such as aimless effort, indolence, combativeness, and contentment with mediocrity.

The development of taste and standards cannot be left to feeling alone. They should be a matter of considerable discussion and consideration, so that preference is brought into conscious recognition. Judgments should be analyzed, not for the purpose of

* See the chart on page 144.

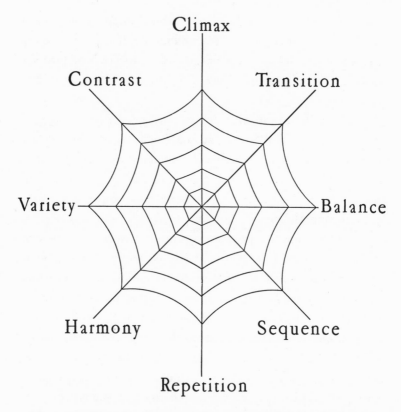

Climax

Contrast   Transition

Variety   Balance

Harmony   Sequence

Repetition

The composing of a dance may be compared to the spinning of a spider web. The pattern is woven from that which is within. In the process, structure is made possible by the medium's being fastened to supporting units (principles of composition). The pattern grows and takes its shape in accordance with inner necessity and the capacity, power, and excellence of execution.

agreement, but for clarification and organization of one's own ideas and for an appreciation of the opinions of others.

When preconceived structural forms are used in too academic and dogmatic a way and superimposed at the expense of direct experience in the creation of organic forms, which are also definite in their way, much valuable experience and satisfaction are denied the student dancer. The use of preconceived forms means that the idea must be forced into an already constructed pattern, whereas organic form is form resulting from the idea's forcing the medium and from a conscious molding and organizing of the materials. Their use depends upon their adequacy to the demands of content. The important point to remember is that any form is significant if it imparts significance to its content.

The delight in proportion, balance, and rhythmic activity is coexistent with human behavior; therefore a dance, as a constructed form, can be a means of both satisfying and experiencing these pleasures. Structural phases of form are sensed as well as understood. They are organic and motor, and are, therefore, emotional because of feelings of balance and unbalanced tensions. Structure in this sense is an organization of forces. Because of these factors, structure has a direct and emotional appeal and therefore adds to clearness of expression and communication. So, if the emotional appeal of structure is in harmony with the emotional demands of content, the two will blend, and meaning will come through uncluttered by the structural scheme.

Composition with the desire to *communicate* as well as to express, that others may share the meanings of a dance, forces the dancer so to fashion and organize and execute his materials that communication may result. No matter how individual and private our feelings may be, when it comes to the expression of them, the dancer is responsible for their modification, that they may be universally communicative. It is one thing to dance alone and for one's own pleasure (of the first importance), but, if a dancer is genuinely interested in projecting his experience for others, he dances in a way that will be both pleasing and convincing. He takes upon himself the task of selecting, organizing, and executing in a way that others may understand. His power to do this will depend upon education, experience, artistic taste and development, personal idiosyncrasies, and creative and technical ability.

The final dance, as art form, is an aggregate of elements. Its development consists of several stages, each with its particular technique. There is the technique of selecting and organizing the psychological elements into substance and content, and the technique of selecting, organizing, and executing the motor elements. All become bound together and made as one by the overflow of rhythm into all phases.

A dance, then, is a definite thing consisting of many parts that are interdependent. It is an embodiment of emotional experience in expressive art movement, upon which the principles of composition are consciously imposed by the personality which was the subject of the experience that is being given expressive form. It is the projection of neural forces within us, whose tensions must of necessity influence the fashioning of the medium into the form of their expression.

FORM AND STRUCTURE

Dance composition is concerned with the way in which inner experience is brought into existence by technique, not only as skillfully executed movements, but as an artful relating and integrating of these movements, so that their organization results in a dance symbolizing unity between content and the form of its expression.

Technique in this broader sense refers to the whole process, mental and physical, which enables the dancer to embody aesthetic experience in a composition, as well as the skill to execute it. *Technique, form,* and *expression* become interdependent aspects of the same thing, for, as soon as an idea or feeling is expressed, it has taken upon itself a form—and form is brought into existence by technique.

Accordingly, as the dancer has a clear and convincing, or a vague and unconvincing, sense of what he is doing, and of what is fitting and technically possible, so will his dance be well or badly formed and executed. Communication depends upon the dancer's sensitivity to the expressive value of his motor symbols and upon his skill as craftsman and performer.

Since expression is essential to dance as art and since the urge to expression is primarily emotional, every dance composition depends for its ultimate value upon the nature of its content. This will vary with the different qualities of each dancer's emotional nature and with his ability to execute in movement. So it follows that there can be no one way of composing nor one style that is absolute. The final form, then, instead of being dominated by dogmatic rules (only as they are pertinent to structural solutions), is determined by the dancer's integrity, which selects and organizes the elements of a dance into patterns that are convincing, pleasing, and meaningful. He is free to use old forms or create new ones according to his artistic integrity and ability.

Because both personal experience and artistic restraint are necessary to expression, it is clear that, no matter what the source of a dancer's initial impulse, it is the richness of experience and the sensitivity of the selecting personality which control and color the material, and which make of movement—a dance.

Schematic Representation of Elements Contributing to Dance

RHYTHMIC FACTORS

- PULSE
- INTERVALS
- DURATION
- STRESS
- SPEED
- METER
- COMPLEX COMBINATIONS
- SYNCOPATION

SPACE FACTORS

- DIRECTION
- FOCUS
- LINE OF MOTION
- DIRECT
- DEVIATING
- DISTANCE OR RANGE
- PLANES
- HORIZONTAL
- VERTICAL
- DIAGONAL
- BODY POSITION
- LEVELS
- HIGH
- LOW
- MEDIUM
- BODY FACING
- FORWARD
- SIDEWARD
- BACKWARD

FORM FACTORS

- VARIETY
- CONTRAST
- BALANCE
- CLIMAX
- SEQUENCE
- TRANSITION
- REPETITION
- HARMONY

TECHNIQUES

- STRENGTH
- FLEXIBILITY
- QUALITY (COORDINATION)
- SPECIFIC SKILLS

A. Anatomical structure sets mechanical limits for motor response. The body is capable of flexion extension, abduction adduction, rotation circumduction, range and the activities of locomotion – walk – run – leap – hop – jump – simple combinations skip – gallop – slide. Their combinations offer an infinite variety of postures, gestures and actions.

B. Physiological determinants of movement are a consideration of physico-chemical processes and the neuro-muscular system. It is a behavior equipment possessing reflex paths and infinite possible activities that can be modified. It is by virtue of this structure that specific technical skills can be emancipated from diffuse responses. It is highly modifiable and must be educated by doing.

C. Mental equipment determines psychic behavior. (Is dependent upon B.) Here resides the awareness of all sensations as well as the capacity to think, feel, imagine, create, etc. It is the equipment for interpreting experience and developing a sense of values. This structure is the formative substance from which emerges personality. It is highly modifiable and educable and needs broad experience. It represents the personal human endowments that through knowledge and use are the only forces that lend warmth and significance to any act.

A.-B.-C. Are the expression of racial and family heredities.

DEPARTMENT OF PHYSICAL EDUCATION FOR WOMEN
UNIVERSITY OF WISCONSIN - MADISON, WISCONSIN
- 1938 -

The chart above is a visible representation of the integration of all the elements that enter into the study of dance.

It is conceived in the form of a loom.

A. The confining outline represents the limitations of movement determined by anatomical structure.

B. The dotted area represents the physiological determinants of movement.

C. The crosses represent the psychical equipment.

B and C form the matrix—that substance of our make-up that furnishes the background which receives impressions and out of which arise, in high relief, personality and patterns of behavior. They form the plastic material that is sensitive and educable.

A, B, and C represent the native equipment which every student brings to the study of dance. The strands of the warp represent movement studies that are entered into for the specific purposes of flexibility, strength, co-ordination, and specific skills; but inherent in them are the elements represented by the woof strands. Each strand is a particular interest that is "pulled out" for special study, so that the student may not only master it as technique but discover what contributions it makes to a larger organization, and how it is in turn affected by the whole of which it is a part.

Chapter 8

DANCE AND MUSIC

*Both dance and music have rhythm
as the basis of their movement.*

A DISCUSSION of dance would be incomplete without some reference to music. It is quite possible to dance without music, and dance should be recognized and experienced as an independent art. But because of the very special and organic relationship of the two arts, much may be gained from building on this relationship and opening the resources of music to the dancer.

Music is said to have come from dance, from the rhythmic impulses of man, and to have taken from dance its rhythmic form and structure. Such an alliance suggests the following development.

The sensations of the varying intensities and stresses and speeds and irregularities of man's powers of locomotion and body exertion must have always delighted and satisfied his inborn sense of rhythm. The agitations of the muscles under strong emotional pressure stimulated the activity of his other natural means of expression. He used his voice; he shouted and yelled and cried. He uttered sounds of joy, sorrow, pain, and fear: the first music. In this stage, music was little more than tone and rhythm. Its rise and fall of pitch, its intensities and accents and tempo, existed as the tonal accompaniment of dance, enhancing and also revealing its emotional expression. Later, man became aware of the power that the sound of his voice had over his emotions, and discovered he could use his voice not only as the language of his feelings but also to arouse an answering state in others, and thus incite to action. As he developed a language, his cries and exclamations became words—thus music grew into song. Because of its new form and completeness as combined in melody and poetry, music severed its connection with dance and became an independent art, leaving dance a free agent of expression. As civilization advanced, words asserted their independence of music, and poetry made its flight into the broad realms of art. Thus three separate arts arose where one had existed. But even though music and poetry have achieved freedom, their rhythmic principles remain those sensed as the motor concomitants of emotional impulses, and as stored kinesthetic memories of past motor experience.

Like all things, music has grown by minute increments. Centuries have faded into the past since the first cry of joy or pain and the first beating of sticks, which marked the rhythms of dance, became fused and elaborated into melody and harmony. It has taken all the resources of man's science and culture to develop the crude rhythms of the first music into the glorious symphonies of the last century. Although dance is older, how young and neglected it seems when compared with the maturity and expansion of music! When man accords to dance the same opportunities and interest he has granted to music, dance too will come into its own and rightly be recognized as an art worthy of sincere effort and study.

Because of its transient phase, music has become associated with movement. And because of the dynamic urge of its rhythmic structure, in addition to its melodic and harmonic qualities, music is the most important of all the partners of the dance. The dancer in his response can translate the sounds he hears back into emotions which will be the substance of a dance. In its purest form, music, like abstract dance, has within its scope only the most generalized emotional situations. It does not depict literally, nor does it require of the listener knowledge of any particular facts. Rather it arouses moods without necessarily arousing associations that impel the mind to make a concrete interpretation. But the listener, if he so desires, may interpret what he hears in concrete imagery.

Although music involves an organization of sound in terms of time and stress values, what is more significant is its melodic and harmonic structure. Rhythmic structure alone has the power of exciting strong feeling states, but it is the melodic and harmonic structures that give music its particular power to express emotions reflecting mental states. In the history of music and dance we find that compositions were written especially to regulate the steps of conventional dances of the period, such as the saraband, the pavan, the gavotte, and others. In these cases, the form of the dance step determined the meter and form of the composition. But music need not be limited to this one relationship. Its literature is so rich in inspiration that, if wisely and artistically used, it has much more to offer. Of all the arts, perhaps music makes the most direct appeal to the emotions.

Music and dance have rhythm as the basis of their movement, and, because of its temporal phase, music is able to express abstract aspects of action. It can suggest or express ease or difficulty of action, its advance or retreat, its force or weakness, its excitement or repose, its seriousness or gaiety. Through association all degrees and qualities of feeling states are expressed and aroused. Music through tone, and dance through movement, give the feeling tones of ideas, things, or events, not the ideas or things or events themselves.

Music, rightly used, offers a justified guidance to dance creation. Especially is this true for the less experienced dancer, whose motor and ideational vocabulary is not adequate to achieving an independent dance. Through rhythmic structure music may guide the rhythmic form of movement responses and give the setting for a mood or idea. Through its time and tempo and intensity gradations it may exert a control over the range and quality of movement—all aiding in the understanding of the similarity in the structure of the two arts.

When a musical composition is used as the source of inspiration for a dance, its structure will necessarily affect the structure of the dance form related to it. At the same time it arouses associative meanings, and with these come personal and subjective responses. Thus, when music inspires a dance, the result is not an entirely new creation but a reproduction, in a different medium, of something that has existed before. The emotion and the basic form are the same, and both the musical composition and the dance process are creative. The music, carrying a meaning, stimulates to a new creative act. This act is a reinterpretation into the form of another art. Thus a dance inspired by music is like any dance, regardless of the source of its original impulse and structural idea.

To accept aid from music intelligently is, after all, an exercise of knowledge essential to the creation of any dance. The dancer recognizes the sources of help and identifies himself with them and incorporates them in his creative process. It makes no difference whether they are marshaled from the memory of past experience or whether he is reminded of them by objective experience in the outside world.

It is dangerous for dance to follow rules of melody that were never intended for bodily movement, but which may nevertheless give rise to it. If dance is not understood and developed independently of music, it is likely to lean too heavily upon music and lose its own vitality. Too great a dependence on music is often due to lack of ability to respond fully to it. A dance should depend upon the dancer's own concepts to impel and control its movements.

A dance thus related to a musical composition is the interpretation of the dancer's emotional and intellectual responses. It is not limited to the literal translation of note values into activity. Associative meanings put emphasis here and restraint there, molding the whole into an artistic and individual response.

The ideal use of music would be to have it composed for the dance as an accompaniment, as an accompaniment for a violin or for the voice is composed. As an accompaniment, it should bring about a musical analogy to the meaning of the dance, rhythmically and emotionally. It should contribute to the dance rather than detract by obtruding. It must keep its place and not bid for attention. The composer should make his music affirmative, but not let his musical ambition cause him to write music that pleases him intellectually and structurally alone. The music should merge with the dance so that its presence is felt by an enhanced total effect and not by individual achievement. As an accompaniment, the music is a means of helping the observer to sense the dancer's thought and feeling, for it is one more sense perception added to the visual and kinesthetic. Unfortunately, it is not possible for every teacher of dance to have such trained and talented musicians for his accompanists. But, if music is selected wisely and used intelligently, we need not despair, for there is much excellent material to be found in musical literature. The association between dance and music is close and natural, and it will continue. If rightly understood and used, their relationship is of great mutual benefit.

Chapter 9

WHY DANCE?

As long as man is responsive to the forces of life and the universe, there will be dance.

LIFE, in all its forms, is a manifestation of a quickening force sensed as energy. Coexistent with this force, and regulating its flow, is the phenomenon of rhythm. Without its principle of order and proportion all would be chaos. Its presence is revealed in the life patterns and forms of all organic processes. Man and everything that he does are subject to its rules of organization. Nothing escapes. Feelings and thoughts, as well as actions, are subject to this rhythmic scheme. Thus dance, itself an expression of organic and bodily rhythm, must be considered as an extension of emotional and intellectual rhythmic form, projected into and through movement. The fact that dance has not perished through the ages is evidence of its value to mankind.

The nature of the modern world makes it imperative that provision for some art experience be made. Our age, for the greater number of people, is one of industrialism and routine. The detail of the office, the piece job and the assembly line of the factory, rob the worker of any opportunity to identify himself with his work. He has no chance to create beauty of form or to share his aesthetic experiences through artistic creation. It is no wonder that he should seek the dance halls and motion pictures, which seem to him the only available means to satisfy, however inadequately, his need for wider expression through vicarious participation. Our civilization does not afford the wealth of opportunity for free and impulsive individual expression possessed by primitive man; we do not have his opportunities for sharing through group expression the thoughts and feelings of our fellows. The progress of civilization has brought the impulse to express feelings too rigidly under the domination of reason, resulting in stylized and mechanized forms and imitative art. This, in turn, has had its influence. It has caused the average individual to think of himself as a perpetual spectator of art, afraid to create his own forms because they seem beyond him. We are, of course, no longer in a primitive stage of culture; primitive forms of expression are not ours—nor can primitive art fully satisfy people of the twentieth century. Yet, when we realize the important role that expressive activities have played at every stage in the evolution of the race, we cannot fail to appreciate the need for them in our lives today.

In no age can man live in his intellect alone. The emotional life of the normal human being must find some outlet and some answering satisfaction from his fellows. The artist lying dormant in him must be allowed to develop. Too often it is pent up within a hard and unresponsive exterior that repels rather than encourages the much desired fellowship of feeling.

It is only recently that the necessity of some form of creative art expression for the healthy mental life has been fully realized. Mental science is revealing more clearly the nature of those deeper emotional tensions that arise when powerful feelings are checked within the mind with no opportunity for expression. Such tension often works havoc, whereas the same emotion understood, and with its energies transferred into another channel, becomes a source of personal power. Repressed feelings often become wasted for want of use, or, finding no refining and transmuting release, they remain powerful and crude, and continue by a kind of underground existence.

Many of our people are cut off from expression by their own

constrained self-consciousness, which blocks any form of free, harmonious expression in the projection of an integrated self-totality. They are embarrassed in the presence of any call to bodily expression. They lack the co-ordination of body and mind with its feeling states, which would permit them to move and act with ease and sureness. Consequently they feel the body to be a liability and an instrument over which there is little control. Every teacher faces this problem in both its forms—the fear of emotional expression, and the imprisonment of the personality in an unresponsive body. Dance, freeing the body from needless inhibitions and breaking down some of the unessential reserves, frees the personality for a wider and more satisfying life.

This physical effectiveness is a resource for the development of personality, for many mental as well as physical elements go into its making. It helps the student to cultivate his sympathies, to refine his taste, and to strengthen his preference for the finer things in both art and life. These are worth-while services, for half the battle of conduct is a sense of values to guide us in our preferences. It is true that dance cannot put into the student what is not already within the scope of his natural powers and interests, but it can help to develop the powers he has in the direction of greater effectiveness.

Every normal person enjoys the exhilaration of vigorous rhythmical movement, whether he is working with a group or by himself, and the sense of power that comes from the exercise of all his faculties in well co-ordinated movements. This pleasure is re-creative in the best meaning of the word. It is a relaxing of unnecessary nervous tension. Such a releasing of undue tension prevents useless expenditure of energy. We relieve that energizing of parts which constitutes an unnecessary drain upon our nerve force. Relaxation, when rightly understood and used, conserves energy by promoting its rhythmical flow through an uninhibited body, thus affording a freshening of interest and energy by bringing about a restoration of depleted powers. And the pleasure in free, vigorous, and rhythmical movement that is essential to the study of dance is the more significant from the point of view of education in that the true dance enthusiast can create its beauty and pleasure for himself.

Of all the art forms, dance is the most generally available, since everyone finds the instrument needed for his purpose in his own body. Anyone who understands how can create his own dance, or find meaning in forms that have been created by others, and so satisfy, to some extent, his latent desire to experience and manifest what is pleasing to him in content and form. For subjectively a dance is an ideal toward which the imaginative mind reaches and in which satisfaction is experienced in the attainment of the ideal; and objectively a dance is a reality so formed that it becomes a symbol of the ideal and a communication of the mind's yearning and satisfaction.

One of the greatest values of any art is its power to carry the individual beyond himself into a broader world of imaginative experience and understanding. The problem of composing an emotional experience into the meaningful movements of a dance makes the student more observant of the people around him—of the rich play of feeling that goes on constantly under the surface of everyday life. In observing and evaluating the life patterns that surround him, he has a chance to become more understanding, more sympathetically respectful of the inner life of others, and so to enter through the gate of his own experience into a universal understanding. At the same time he enriches his own emotional life.

And, further, dance not only satisfies and deepens the aesthetic sense by its own forms, but also gives insight into the fundamental elements common to all the arts. It carries the student beyond the limits of one art into the wider realm of all art and makes him a citizen of its world of beauty and meaning. This is a valuable service, for it ministers to one of man's oldest and most persistent needs. The history of the arts is the story of man's love for the beautiful, of his search for the harmonies of form and meaning which will satisfy his yearning for the ideal.

But even more important for this wider orientation than the knowledge of beauty is the attitude which the dance helps to cultivate, for the accessibility to any art experience depends upon the aesthetic attitude with which it is approached. The most significant characteristic of this attitude, as we have seen, is a detached, impersonal relation to the object observed. It is a "psychic distance" whereby the observer is enabled to appreciate the object as an object, judging it solely by its own appropriate standards. Obviously, the aesthetic attitude demands a considerable evolution and education of the personal capacities. It is apparent that it reaches beyond art in the narrower sense. For, as was also brought out in an earlier chapter, there are few experiences in life which do not possess elements of beauty. We are so apt to think that only the fine arts contain these elements that we need to make the effort to remember and discover that they may be present in many of the events that just happen during the course of the day. The possessor of the aesthetic attitude is aware of this fact and recognizes these elements wherever he finds them. It releases his energies for co-operation with like-minded fellows in the creation and appreciation of art. This attitude toward art and life is the greatest contribution of dance to the larger aims of education.

But of what particular value is such a creative art study?

Because the materials of art are derived from reality, the integration of thought, feeling, and action which is present in a dance has a direct relationship with life itself and the life of the creator, which was its source. Increased understanding expressed in art is the counterpart of increased understanding in the mental life of the student. This fuller-developed personality forms a basis for the next art experience. Thus increased understanding is constantly revealed in successive stages of his creations.

Composition affords opportunity to experience the value of sincerity and simplicity. It requires the study of principles and a sincere effort to seek out inner meanings. In abstracting material for a dance from his fund of experience, the student learns that the mere expression of his own peculiarities is poor material out of which to create art. In the same way he learns that dances of more communal expression, whose themes have a wider validity, make a more interesting dance for the enjoyment of others. He learns that there is no substitute for sincerity and genuineness. The student's composition may not be good from the professional critics' standpoint, but it is his own. Psychologically speaking, his creation may answer to as great a need for expression as that of the artist dancer.

The source of all art is the individual personality. The dancer, when creating, is forced to face the content of his own personality and make selections from it. He experiences an awakening and refining of the excellencies of his nature which may ultimately affect everyday living. He seeks to identify himself with the ideal meaning of his experiences, and in his attempt to do so he is led to the exercise of critical judgment and discrimination. In his efforts to compose, the student develops an appreciation of the compositions of greater artists, and also knows the joy of achieving something of his own.

In the effort to attain unity in expression, the emotional nature is brought under control and given the strength of restraint. The personality is active in its entirety, unified and expanded in experiencing a perfect form of expression. Thus every dance is born of the personality and gives back to the personality. It brings form, integration, and enrichment.

As in the creation of a dance, so in life, one of the main problems is that of harmonizing the multitudinous contributing elements. The dancer who has understood the process of composition should be able to carry over his knowledge into a technique of artistic living. In creating a style of life, one is ever searching for ways to become more sensitive to the many stimuli that con-

DANCE: A CREATIVE ART EXPERIENCE

stantly bombard mankind, seeking how best to evaluate and select experiences and meanings, and trying to organize these innumerable and conflicting elements into coherent patterns of behavior that reveal a life well integrated and adjusted to its environment, which, when all is said, is any one man's greatest art achievement. The contribution dance can make to such living is its primary value to an individual life and to society.

The fact that there has always been dance compels us to accept it as an old and deeply rooted human activity whose foundations reside in the nature of man. It will continue as long as the rhythmic flow of energy operates, and until man ceases to respond to the forces of life and the universe. As long as there is life, there will be dance.

> 'Tis to create, and in creating live
> A being more intense, that we endow with form
> Our fancy, gaining as we give
> The life we image.
>
> Lord Byron